Good Housekeeping

grilling

More than 120 Perfect Year-Round Recipes

Tex-Mex Burgers, page 38

Good Housekeeping
grilling

**More than 120 Perfect
Year-Round Recipes**

HEARST BOOKS
A division of Sterling Publishing Co., Inc.

New York / London
www.sterlingpublishing.com

GOOD HOUSEKEEPING
Rosemary Ellis, *Editor in Chief*
Susan Westmoreland, *Food Director*
Samantha Cassetty, M.S., R.D., *Nutrition Director*
Sharon Franke, *Kitchen Appliances and Technology Director*

Book Design: Anna Christian
Project Editor: Pamela Hoenig
Production Editor: Sarah Scheffel
Photography Credits on page 139

Library of Congress Cataloging-in-Publication Data

Good housekeeping grilling : more than 275 perfect year-round recipes.
    p. cm.
 ISBN 978-1-58816-714-9
1. Barbecuing. I. Good housekeeping (New York, N.Y.)
II. Title: Grilling.
 TX840.B3G66 2011
 641.7'6—dc22

                    2010028170

The Good Housekeeping Cookbook Seal guarantees that the recipes in this cookbook meet the strict standards of the Good Housekeeping Research Institute. The Institute has been a source of reliable information and a consumer advocate since 1900, and established its seal of approval in 1909. Every recipe has been triple-tested for ease, reliability, and great taste.

Published by Hearst Books
A division of Sterling Publishing Co., Inc.
387 Park Avenue South, New York, NY 10016

Good Housekeeping is a registered trademark of Hearst Communications, Inc.
www.goodhousekeeping.com

For information about custom editions, special sales, premium and corporate purchases, please contact Sterling Special Sales Department at 800-805-5489 or specialsales@sterlingpublishing.com.

Distributed in Canada by Sterling Publishing
c/o Canadian Manda Group, 165 Dufferin Street
Toronto, Ontario, Canada M6K 3H6

Distributed in Australia by
Capricorn Link (Australia) Pty. Ltd.
P.O. Box 704, Windsor, NSW 2756 Australia

Manufactured in China

This special edition was printed for Kohl's Department Stores, Inc. (for distribution on behalf of Kohl's Cares, LLC, its wholly owned subsidiary) by Hearst Books, a division of Sterling Publishing Co., Inc.

ISBN 978-1-61837-028-0

KOHL'S
ISBN 978-1-61837-028-0
Factory Number: 123386
02/12

10 9 8 7 6 5 4 3 2 1

Tomato, Portobello, and Mozzarella Melts, page 28

Lemon Chicken with Grilled Summer Squash, page 53

Contents

Foreword

For Americans, grilling is not just a cooking method, it's an event. We savor the enticing aromas and incomparable flavors of a backyard barbecue and have extended the grilling season long beyond those summer events. In recent years, grilling has become a bit of a phenomenon, being touted as a great way to cook by everyone from chefs to dieticians. Though they may endorse grilled food for different reasons, there is no denying that juicy steaks and burgers, fresh vegetables, chicken, seafood, and even pizzas, all taste better when enhanced by the intense heat and savory smoke of the grill. Couple that with amazing ease and versatility and it's clear why grilling is everyone's favorite cooking method. But the best news is you can enjoy luscious grilled food year round. Whether you grill in a hat and gloves (or under an umbrella!) in inclement weather, or prepare one of our outstanding grill pan recipes from the comfort of your kitchen, we

provide the know-how—and more than 120 delectable, triple-tested recipes.

But before you start your grill, bone up on essential tools, techniques, and safety procedures by reviewing "The Way to Great Grilling" on page 10. We discuss the different types of grills—the foolproof gas grill (the favorite of most backyard griller's today), the traditional charcoal grill, and the latest thing in grilling, the electric grill, which allows you to cook without an open flame, so it's perfect for a small deck or patio. An overview of grilling baskets and skewers, instant-read thermometers and a variety of fire starters will help you pick the right gear, and our tips on lighting and maintaining proper heat will help ensure great results. If you want to imbue your food with even more aroma, check out our tips on flavoring the fire. The grill pan is so fast and easy to use, it has become a favorite tool in the weeknight (and dieters') repertoire. Follow our advice on getting the most from your grill pan to enjoy equally delicious grilled meals on those days when you want grilled flavor without stepping outside.

Recipes start with crowd-pleasing appetizers—from quesadillas to chicken saté to wings—you'll be delighted to serve these at any soirée. Pesto and Mozzarella Pizzas are proof that the grill is ideal for preparing pizzas. And, of course, because burgers are everyone's favorite grilled food, we offer a variety of juicy takes, from beef to BLT, many of which can be made in a grill pan.

But the meat of this cookbook is the entrées: Some, like Chicken with Gremolata Salsa and Hoisin-Glazed Pork Tenderloin, are ideal for easy weeknight suppers. Korean-Style Short Ribs, Sweet and Tangy BBQ Chicken, and Spiced Grilled Tuna on Spinach Salad require a bit more time, which makes them just right for a leisurely weekend barbecue. Our recipes for rubs, sauces, and salsas will add mouthwatering flavor to even a simple chicken breast. Vegetables and sides are stars on the grill, too: Whether you want to grill a platter of veggies or serve up Hot Buttered Chili-Lime Corn, we've got you covered. So fire up your grill (or grill pan) and enjoy our triple-tested recipes year round!

—Susan Westmoreland
Food Director, *Good Housekeeping*

The Way to Great Grilling—Outdoors and In

Whether you cook on a shoebox-size hibachi or in a state-of-the-art gas grill with side burners and an infrared rotisserie, you know that grilling imparts an incomparable flavor that no other cooking method can. The intense heat, the savory smoke, and the pleasure of cooking (and eating) outdoors all enhance the natural flavor of top-grade steaks, plump chicken breasts, sparkling seafood, and garden-fresh vegetables.

Before you fire up your grill, spend a few minutes with these pages to assess your grill and utensils, bone up on techniques and flavor-enhancing tricks, and review safety procedures.

TYPES OF GRILLS

Whether you prefer to cook on a gas, charcoal, or electric grill (and some avid grillers own more than one type of grill), manufacturers are now offering consumers an enticing array of options to choose from.

Gas Grills

Offering speed and ease of operation, the gas grill has become America's favorite type of grill. And what's not to like? Open the gas valve, turn on the controls, preheat for about 10 minutes, and you're ready to go. With gas grills—fueled by either liquid propane or natural gas—you've got a world of features to choose from, including:

■ a wide range of BTU capacities, up to almost 50,000 BTUs, depending on the manufacturer

■ stainless steel, cast-iron (holds the heat better for a superior sear), or porcelain-coated cooking grates (makes for easy clean-up)

■ stainless steel or porcelain-coated

flavor bars (V-shaped bars that catch dripping fat and return it to the cooking food in the form of tasty smoke)

■ infrared burners for searing

■ side burners that allow you to do stovetop cooking while you grill

■ a special lower-BTU smoker burner, as well as a smoker box for wood chips

■ a rotisserie burner and attachment

■ a warming rack, which allows you to stop food from cooking as soon as it's done

■ built-in grill thermometers, grill lights, and storage

In terms of size, you can find a gas grill to fit your needs, whether you're cooking for one or the entire neighborhood.

Charcoal Grills

Fueled by charcoal briquettes or natural hardwood charcoal chunks, charcoal grills are, on the whole, less expensive than their gas-powered brethren. Look for a charcoal grill made of heavy-gauge steel; a porcelain-enamel coating will give you better protection from rust. Look for sturdy legs positioned to keep the grill steady. Other features you can look for in a charcoal grill include:

■ plated steel, preseasoned cast-iron, or porcelain-enameled cooking grates

■ adjustable-height fire grates

■ side shelves and bottom storage

■ warming rack

■ temperature gauge

■ removable ash trays for easy cleaning

As with gas grills, you can find a charcoal grill to fit your needs. If you're cooking for one or two, consider the hibachi, a small cast-iron grill that's just right for a pocket-sized patio.

Electric Grill

The electric grill offers an alternative to messing around with propane tanks and charcoal. Plug it in and you're good to go. Or, if you live where charcoal or gas is not allowed on the terrace, patio, or deck, there are tabletop versions as well as full-size electric grills available; just be sure to position your grill within reach of a grounded outlet.

OTHER EQUIPMENT

Cooking over fire calls for some specialized tools, and there are also optional gadgets to consider for easier grilling of fish, kabobs, and so on. Here are the basics, plus some extras:

GRILL TOPPER: If you often grill delicate foods such as seafood and vegetables, you'll want a grill topper, a perforated metal sheet or tray that provides a nearly smooth surface for grilling. Food is less likely to break up or fall through, and you can virtually "stir-fry" cut-up foods over the flames.

GRILLING BASKETS: This is another option for delicate or small foods. There are classic fish-shaped baskets (which hold whole fish) as well as square and oblong baskets with long handles to hold kabobs, baby vegetables, or fish fillets. Once the food is inside and the basket is clamped shut, you can turn the entire thing at once—easy!

TONGS: Better than a fork for turning foods, because they don't pierce the surface and release juices. Barbecue tongs should have heatproof handles and rounded ends that won't cut into the food.

SPATULA: Use one with a long, heatproof handle for flipping burgers and moving food around on a grill topper.

SKEWERS: Long metal skewers are a must for kabobs. Choose skewers with flat shafts rather than round ones; food will be less likely to slip or spin around as you turn the skewers.

BASTING BRUSH: A heatproof handle and a long shaft are two definite brush requirements. As for bristles, silicone is the way to go—it's nearly indestructible and has the added benefit of being nonstick, making cleanup a snap. Your next best bet is a brush with natural bristles, which will stand up to heat better than synthetic bristles other than silicone.

THERMOMETERS: Consider two different types of thermometers for grilling ease. The first measures the internal temperature of the food you're cooking (see "Is It Done?," page 15). You

can do this with an instant-read thermometer (available as a dial or a battery-powered digital probe), which is inserted into the center of the food when you think it's getting close to done. Another alternative is a thermometer that consists of a probe that is inserted into the food as it goes onto the grill, which is attached to a digital readout that sits outside the grill.

The other kind of thermometer is a grill surface thermometer, which measures the heat of the fire. When you're cooking with charcoal, it takes the guesswork out of determining whether you've got a hot or medium fire (see "How Hot Is Your Fire?," opposite). It's especially useful when you're cooking "low and slow," which requires maintaining an even temperature over many hours.

GRILLING MITTS: A more serious version of oven mitts, these are longer and better insulated, to protect more of your arm from higher heat. Heavy suede mitts are excellent.

BRASS-BRISTLED SCRUB BRUSH: Use this to clean the grill rack. The best time for this? While the grill is still hot.

FOR THE FIRE

Gas and electric grills are easy to light; just follow the manufacturer's directions. A charcoal fire requires a little more finesse. Be sure to leave enough time after starting the fire for the coals to develop a light layer of ash before you start cooking. Allow 20 minutes to be on the safe side.

Getting Started on Your Charcoal Grill

You don't want to run out of heat before your food is cooked, so start with enough briquettes. Estimate the right amount by spreading an even layer over the bottom of the firebox. Before lighting, stack them into a pyramid to allow air to circulate among them. The following are options to help you get the fire going:

CHIMNEY STARTER: This is an open-ended metal cylinder with a handle. Stuff crumpled newspaper in the bottom of it, fill the top portion with briquettes, then light the paper through an opening in the bottom. The briquettes will burn to ash-covered readiness.

ELECTRIC STARTER: A loop-shaped heating element with a handle, this device is placed in a bed of briquettes; plug it in and the briquettes will ignite.

LIQUID FIRE STARTER: Saturate briquettes with the liquid, then wait for a minute before lighting. By the time the coals are ready for proper cooking, the fluid will have burned off and will not affect the flavor of the food. Never add liquid starter to a fire that's already burning or to hot coals; a spark could ignite the whole can.

SOLID FIRE STARTER: Place these waxy-looking cubes in the firebox, pile briquettes on top, and light. They're safer to handle than liquid starter.

SELF-STARTING BRIQUETTES: These are impregnated with starter fluid. A match will ignite them immediately. Don't add them to a fire that's already lit.

HOW HOT IS YOUR FIRE?

You'll know the coals are ready when they are about 80 percent ashy gray (at night, you'll see them glow red). To test the level of heat, hold your palm above the coals at cooking height (about 6 inches): If you can keep your palm over the fire for just 2 to 3 seconds, the fire is hot (above 375°F); 4 to 5 seconds, the fire is medium (above 300°F); 5 to 6 seconds, the fire is low (above 200°F).

Tapping the coals will remove their ash cover and make the fire hotter. Pushing the coals together intensifies the heat; spreading them apart decreases it. Opening the vents on a covered grill increases the temperature, and partially closing them lowers the heat.

8 Safety Rules
for the Backyard Chef

1. Make sure the grill is on a level surface and not too close to the house, trees, fences, or even deck railings—all can catch fire from flare-ups or flying sparks.

2. Don't line the bottom of a gas or charcoal grill with aluminum foil; it will obstruct airflow, and the fire will die out faster.

3. Use lighter fluid only to start a fire; don't squirt it onto hot coals to get a dying fire going again, because it can ignite in the can as you pour it.

4. We can't say it too often: Reduce the risk of cross contamination and food poisoning by transferring cooked food from the grill to a clean plate, not one that held raw meat, fish, or poultry.

5. Boil used marinades and glazes for 1 minute if you want to serve them with cooked meat. Or reserve some in a separate dish before it comes in contact with the meat, fish, or poultry.

6. Use long-handled barbecue utensils (not your regular kitchen set) for good reach and control. And watch out for dangling sleeves.

7. Be careful not to serve undercooked meat, poultry, or fish. (See "Is It Done?," opposite, for guidelines.)

8. Don't throw water on flare-ups; it produces steam vapors, which can cause severe burns. Instead, remove the food from the grill until the fire subsides or cover the grill for a few minutes. To prevent flare-ups, trim excess fat from meats.

Choose Your Cooking Method

One of the keys to successful grilling is cooking over the right kind of heat—direct or indirect—over the right level heat for the food you're preparing. Here's a primer to get you started.

DIRECT COOKING: The gas grill is preheated with all the burners on or, in a charcoal grill, the prepared coals are spread evenly. Food is placed on the grill rack directly over the heat source. This method works best with foods that take less than 25 minutes, such as steaks, chops, and vegetables. Direct heat is necessary for searing, which gives meats that nice crusty surface.

INDIRECT COOKING: Place your food on the grill rack of a gas grill, over the drip pan. Preheat the burners on the two outer sides for a three-burner grill (or on one side for a two-burner grill). Set the food over the unheated burner. For a charcoal grill, push the briquettes to the edges of the kettle and place a drip pan in the middle before placing your food on the rack. Indirect cooking is best for longer-cooking meats such as roasts and whole chickens or turkeys, or for delicate foods like fish fillets that might be scorched or dried out by direct heat. Consider placing the food in a pan rather than directly on the grill rack.

IS IT DONE?

The best way to know if your food is done is to measure its internal temperature. Below are the temperatures, as determined by the USDA, that you want you food to register before taking it off the grill. Temperatures should be taken in the thickest part of the food; the thermometer should not touch bone, fat, or gristle.

Chicken breasts and whole poultry	165°F
Ground beef	160°F
Pork	160°F
Fish	145°F
Beef steaks and roasts	145°F
Lamb steaks, ribs, or leg	145°F

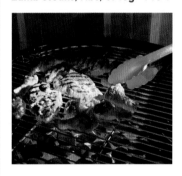

TO COVER OR NOT TO COVER? Most grill manufacturers—both gas and charcoal—recommend closing the cover for all grilling. It reduces flare-ups, helps prevent charring, and greatly shortens cooking time.

HIGH VERSUS MEDIUM HEAT: Use high or medium-high heat for thin cuts of meat that cook quickly: skirt steak, thin pork or lamb chops, frankfurters, or shrimp and other shellfish. Use medium heat for $3/4$- to 1-inch-thick rib-eye, tenderloin, or flank steaks; hamburgers; chicken parts; vegetables; fruit; or whole fish. It's a good idea to sear thick steaks over high heat first, then reduce the heat so the meat can cook through. In all of our recipes, we indicate what level of heat to use.

MAINTAINING PROPER HEAT: For long, slow cooking, you may need to adjust the controls on your gas grill. It's a bit trickier with a charcoal model. If the fire is too hot, close or partially close vents (top, bottom, or both); if it's not hot enough, open the vents fully or add more briquettes after each additional hour as the manufacturer recommends. Most gas and some charcoal grills have thermometers that permit you to monitor the interior temperature without lifting the lid (uncovering causes the temperature to drop very quickly).

FLAVORING THE FIRE

It's the delicious taste of food cooked over flames that makes grilling such a popular cooking method. You can enhance the effect by adding flavor to the fire itself, or, more specifically, the smoke that rises from it. This works best in a covered grill, which holds the smoke in. Aromatic woods, such as mesquite or hickory, are well known for the tang they add to grilled meats. Herbs, spices, and other cooking ingredients add their own flavors.

Grilling woods are sold in chunks or chips to be tossed onto a charcoal fire or into foil packets or the smoker box of a gas grill. You want the wood to smoke slowly, not burn quickly, so soak it in water before adding it. Chips require about half an hour of soaking; larger chunks should be soaked for up to two hours. Here's how to suit the wood to the food:

■ Use oak and mesquite, which are strongly flavored, for cooking beef and pork; their smoke can overpower poultry and seafood.

■ Hickory's sweetness is well suited to turkey, chicken, and pork.

■ Fruitwoods, such as apple and cherry, are mild enough to use with chicken and seafood.

If you've got a gas grill, use wood chips, not chunks. If your gas grill doesn't have a smoker box, wrap the chips up in heavy-duty foil, punch a few holes in it, and place it over the flavor bars.

If you're using a charcoal grill, add chunks of wood to the fire from the start; place chips on the coals later in the cooking process.

Dried grapevines give off a subtle wine flavor, and corncobs (dried for a few days after you've cut the kernels off) produce a hickory-like smoke. Partially cracked nuts in the shell, soaked for 15 minutes or so, release their flavors when heated.

Whole spices or fresh or dried herbs can be placed in the smoker box or on the fire to complement the seasonings in a rub (see page 132). Soak them for about 30 minutes before using. Fennel is traditional for grilling fish, while rosemary, thyme, bay leaves, and cilantro are other options. Experiment with other smoke flavorings, such as whole cinnamon sticks or cloves, strips of orange or lemon peel, and whole garlic cloves.

ENTERTAINING OUTDOORS

For many of us, grilling is a year-round proposition, but grilling really comes into its own when you can enjoy the fire-roasted fruits of your labors outdoors. And when you're planning a patio party or barbecue bash, there's no reason not to approach it as you would an indoor shindig and let your personal style shine through. Here are some pointers for your next outdoor soiree from our own *Good Housekeeping* staff:

■ Plant an old wooden tool caddy with potted herbs for a centerpiece.

■ Fill antique bottles with field flowers— arrange five in the middle of the table or put a bottle at each place setting.

■ Press rosemary, basil, or wildflowers such as Queen Anne's lace under the glass of a large picture frame to make a serving tray.

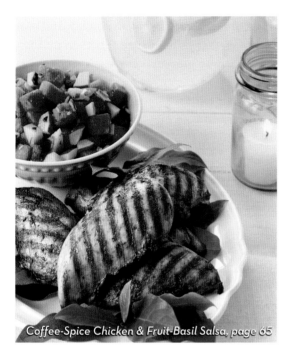
Coffee-Spice Chicken & Fruit-Basil Salsa, page 65

■ Arrange long flatbread crackers in an enamel pail or child's beach pail.

■ Offer bread and cheese on a tray covered with pretty leaves. Just make sure they aren't poisonous (mint and basil are good choices)!

■ For dessert, fill a rustic wooden box with four kinds of cookies, and serve with vanilla ice cream. Or tuck a homemade pound cake with sliced fruit into the box.

■ Use colorful cotton dish towels for napkins. Slide cookie cutters (such as butterflies or flowers) over the rolled towels for napkin rings.

■ Place forks, knives, and spoons in small, clean terra-cotta flowerpots.

■ Use miniature pepper or cherry tomato plants as centerpieces.

■ Pour lemonade into old mason jars or retro soda-fountain glasses. To frost glasses, pop them in the freezer for a few hours.

■ Arrange grilled meat on platters lined with banana leaves (sold fresh or frozen in Asian and Hispanic markets) or green-onion tops.

■ Serve dips in a hollowed-out cabbage or radicchio head, or a scooped-out crusty bread round. Cut the top off to make it level, then spoon out the insides, leaving a $3/4$-inch-thick border all around so the dip doesn't soak through. (Don't fill bread more than 1 hour ahead of time.)

■ If it's really buggy out, stow everything from barbecue chicken to potato salad to pie in picnic baskets on the table and keep them closed while everyone's eating.

■ Make a colorful, edible centerpiece: peaches, nectarines, and plums, with a sprinkle of berries, arranged in a footed glass bowl.

■ Chill water, soda, seltzer, wine, and beer in old galvanized-steel tubs filled with ice.

NOT GUILTY!

Concerned about taking salads or sandwiches made with mayonnaise on a picnic because the mayo might spoil? You're blaming the wrong ingredient: Mayo has a clean record. The rumors began decades ago with homemade mayonnaise, which contains raw eggs; commercial brands, made with pasteurized eggs, have a high acid content (they contain vinegar and lemon juice) that actually prevents the growth of food-poisoning bacteria. The real culprits? Low-acid salad ingredients and sandwich fillings, such as tuna, ham, chicken, eggs, potatoes, and macaroni. When mishandled (left unrefrigerated too long or prepared with hands or utensils that have not been washed properly), they can encourage bacterial growth, even if dressed with mayo.

GOING MOBILE

Want to take your grilling on the road for a picnic at a park? Here are some tips for efficient packing and food safety when you have to leave your refrigerator behind.

■ Gingham-trimmed baskets are romantic, but they won't keep food cold. You need a cooler—and it should be the right size. A full cooler keeps food cold longer than a partially empty one. (If necessary, pack empty space with ice or frozen juice boxes.)

■ For the ultimate in cool, prechill carriers (especially beverage holders) by filling them with ice water and pouring it out just before packing.

■ A cooler can't chill foods that aren't already cold. To be sure foods and drinks are completely cold before stowing, refrigerate them until the last minute. Make dressed salads and cooked meats the night before.

■ To keep things neat and clean at the picnic, do as much prep as possible at home. Wash fruit and lettuce, and pat dry. Shape burgers, cut tomato and onion rounds, slice cheese. Remove chicken or steak from store wrappings, pat dry, and season as desired.

■ Double-bag raw meat, poultry, and seafood—whether it's marinated or not—in zip-tight plastic bags to prevent juices from contaminating other food.

■ Put ice packs next to perishables like chicken and cold cuts, but don't place them directly on top of fragile greens, vegetables, or fruits, which can freeze and then wilt, even through their wrappings.

■ At the grill, have a clean plate on hand for cooked foods. Discard any unused marinade or glaze that's touched raw meat or poultry.

■ Once you've finished eating, pack up the buffet. Discard foods left outdoors for more than two hours. Cold cuts, which are especially sensitive to heat, shouldn't be left out longer than thirty minutes. Refrigerate leftovers as soon as you get home.

GRILLING INDOORS

Even if you're an intrepid, all-weather sort of grillmeister, sometimes grilling outdoors just isn't an option—or you'd simply prefer to get your grill on indoors. But that doesn't mean you can't still enjoy the great taste of grilled food. When you think indoors, think grill pan.

A grill pan is a essentially a skillet with ridges in the bottom. Grill pans come in a wide range of sizes, including griddle-style pans without sides built for cooking over two stovetop burners at once—very useful when you're cooking food for more than two people. You've also got your choice of materials, from the classic cast iron and enameled cast iron to stainless steel and hard-anodized aluminum. One thing to consider when purchasing a grill pan is whether you want a stay-cool handle. If you opt for one without that feature, please remember that the handle will get just as hot as the rest of the pan, so don't absentmindedly grab it. If you do, you'll end up with a nasty burn on the palm of your hand.

We do not recommend buying a grill pan with a nonstick coating; these should not be pre-heated empty and if they are heated over more than medium heat, the coating can begin to degrade, releasing harmful chemicals. Seasoned cast iron pans are naturally nonstick. Whether you've seasoned your pan or you've bought it pre-seasoned from the factory, all you need to clean it after each use is a rinse in hot water and a good scrubbing with a stiff brush—no detergent, as that can remove the seasoning. Immediately dry your pan to keep it from rusting. And if it does develop rust, just tackle it with a scouring pad, rinse well, towel dry, and reseason it.

So, can you prepare anything you cook on an outdoor grill in a grill pan? No, but there's an awful lot you can do—all manner of steaks, burgers, lamb, veal, and pork chops, fish steaks and fillets, scallops and shrimp, boneless chicken breasts, and turkey cutlets. Vegetables and greens work too—try whole endive, radicchio, and romaine, as well as asparagus, strips or rings of bell peppers, and thick slices of veggies like squash, eggplant, and fennel. You can also pan-grill slices of pineapple, or peach, plum, or nectarine halves. And try using your grill pan to toast bread for bruschetta.

Grilled Salmon with Herb-Caper Cream, page 114

You can also use your grill pan to make grilled sandwiches or panini. Usually you see people making these on a contact grill or panini press, but a grill pan works just fine. To weight the sandwiches down, you can either set another, smaller, cast-iron pan on top of the sandwiches, or invest in a device that is also, confusingly, called a panini press, a heavy, flat piece of cast iron with a handle.

We've sprinkled an assortment of grill pan recipes throughout the book, and whenever possible, we offer grill pan variations—including lots of great burgers you can grill up on your stovetop. From Cubano Quesadillas and Croque Monsieur to Stuffed Veal Chops and Coriander Steak with Warm Corn Salad, these easy-to-execute recipes all boast great grilled flavor.

Whether you're inside or outdoors, happy grilling!

Appetizers, Pizza, and Sandwiches

Nothing says "patio party" like finger foods and tasty tidbits hot off the grill. We've supplied you with a delicious array of easy-to-put together starters with oh-so-big flavors. You could even forget the main course and make it a party of appetizers! If you haven't tried pizza on the grill yet, you are in for a surprise. Making use of store-bought pizza dough, these recipes take about 20 minutes to put together and require only five minutes on the grill to yield wood-fired flavor you'll never forget. Serve to your family for dinner, or cut them into small pieces and offer them up as appetizers at your next get-together.

How can you make a tasty sandwich even better? Put it on a grill and watch foccacia or sourdough or country-style bread turn golden brown, while your choice of cheese gets all melty and mingles with the other ingredients between the two slices.

Grilled Corn and Jack Quesadillas, page 23

Grilled Pitas with Caramelized Onions and Goat Cheese

Long, slow cooking makes onions very sweet. The onions can be cooked up to three days ahead—just bring them to room temperature before spooning the goat cheese on top.

PREP: 45 minutes   **GRILL:** about 3 minutes
MAKES: 8 appetizer servings

4   tablespoons olive oil
2   jumbo (1 pound each) onions, coarsely chopped
1   teaspoon sugar
¼   teaspoon salt
¼   teaspoon dried tarragon
¼   teaspoon dried thyme
4   (6-inch) pitas, split horizontally in half
6 to 7 ounces soft goat cheese, crumbled
1   tablespoon chopped fresh parsley

1. In nonstick 12-inch skillet, heat 2 tablespoons oil over medium heat. Add onions, sugar, and salt. Cook, stirring frequently, until very soft, about 15 minutes. Reduce heat to medium-low and cook, stirring frequently, until onions are golden brown, about 20 minutes longer.

2. Prepare outdoor grill for direct grilling over low heat.

3. In cup, stir together remaining 2 tablespoons oil, tarragon, and thyme. Brush cut sides of pitas with herb mixture. Spread with goat cheese, then top with caramelized onions.

4. Place pitas, topping side up, on grill rack and grill until bottoms are crisp and topping is heated through, about 3 minutes.

5. To serve, sprinkle with parsley and cut each pita into 4 wedges.

EACH SERVING: About 245 calories, 8g protein, 27g carbohydrate, 12g total fat (4g saturated), 10mg cholesterol, 310mg sodium

> **TIP:** For a tasty variation, try this with whole-wheat pitas, crumbled feta cheese, and fresh snipped dill.

Grilled Corn and Jack Quesadillas

These quesadillas make a fun and simple summer appetizer. To save time, grate the cheese for the quesadillas while the corn is grilling. For photo, see page 20.

PREP: 15 minutes plus cooling
GRILL: about 12 minutes

MAKES: 8 appetizer servings

3   large ears corn, husks and silk removed
4   (8- to 10-inch) low-fat flour tortillas
1   cup shredded reduced-fat Monterey Jack cheese (4 ounces)
½   cup mild or medium-hot salsa
2   green onions, thinly sliced

1. Prepare outdoor grill for covered direct grilling over medium-high heat.

2. Place corn on hot grill rack. Cover grill and cook corn, turning frequently, until brown in spots, 10 to 15 minutes.

3. Transfer corn to plate; set aside until cool enough to handle. When cool, with sharp knife, cut kernels from cobs.

4. Place tortillas on work surface. Evenly divide Monterey Jack, salsa, green onions, and corn on half of each tortilla. Fold tortilla over filling to make 4 quesadillas.

5. Place quesadillas on hot grill rack. Grill, turning once, until browned on both sides, 1 to 2 minutes. Transfer to cutting board; cut each quesadilla into 4 pieces.

EACH SERVING: About 165 calories, 8g protein, 16g carbohydrate, 5g total fat (2.5g saturated), 10mg cholesterol, 470mg sodium

Cubano Quesadillas

The delicious flavors of a Cuban sandwich in a quesadilla!

PREP: 15 minutes   GRILL: 2 to 3 minutes
MAKES: 8 appetizer servings

8   (6-inch) low-fat flour tortillas
¼   cup yellow mustard
4   ounces thinly sliced Black Forest ham
8   sandwich-cut dill pickle slices
4   ounces thinly sliced roast pork from the deli
4   ounces thinly sliced part-skim Swiss cheese

1. Prepare outdoor grill for direct grilling over medium heat.

2. Brush 1 side of each tortilla with mustard. Evenly divide ham, pickles, pork, and Swiss cheese on 4 tortillas. Cover with remaining tortillas, pressing firmly.

3. With large metal spatula, place quesadillas on hot grill rack and cook until tortillas are browned and cheese melts, 2 to 3 minutes, carefully turning over once.

4. Transfer quesadillas to large cutting board; let stand 1 minute. To serve, cut each quesadilla into 4 wedges.

EACH SERVING: About 190 calories, 15g protein, 18g carbohydrate, 6g total fat (2g saturated), 27mg cholesterol, 640mg sodium

Thai Chicken Saté

This take on saté features chicken marinated in curried coconut milk and teamed with pickled cucumbers. The creamy peanut sauce is kicked up with jalapeño.

PREP: 45 minutes   GRILL: 5 to 8 minutes
MAKES: 6 appetizer servings

1	English (seedless) cucumber, thinly sliced crosswise
1½	teaspoons salt
1	tablespoon Thai green curry paste
¼	cup plus ⅓ cup well-stirred unsweetened coconut milk (not cream of coconut)
4	medium skinless, boneless chicken breast halves (about 1¼ pounds total), each cut diagonally into 6 strips
¼	cup creamy peanut butter
2	teaspoons soy sauce
1	teaspoon packed dark brown sugar
⅛	teaspoon ground red pepper (cayenne)
1	tablespoon hot water
¼	cup rice vinegar
3	tablespoons granulated sugar
2	medium shallots, thinly sliced
1	jalapeño chile, seeded and minced
12	(12-inch) metal skewers

1. In medium bowl, toss cucumber with salt; let stand 30 minutes at room temperature.

2. In another bowl, stir together curry paste and ¼ cup coconut milk until blended. Add chicken and turn to coat. Let stand 15 minutes at room temperature, stirring occasionally.

3. Prepare outdoor grill for direct grilling over medium heat.

4. Meanwhile, prepare peanut sauce: In small bowl, with wire whisk, mix peanut butter, soy sauce, brown sugar, ground red pepper, remaining ⅓ cup coconut milk, and hot water until blended and smooth. Transfer sauce to serving bowl. Makes about ⅔ cup.

5. Drain cucumber, discarding liquid in bowl. Pat cucumber dry with paper towels. Return cucumber to bowl; stir in vinegar, granulated sugar, shallots, and jalapeño; cover and refrigerate until ready to serve.

6. Thread 2 chicken strips, accordion-style, on each of 12 metal skewers; discard marinade. Place skewers on hot grill rack. Cover grill and cook, turning skewers once, just until chicken loses its pink color throughout, 5 to 8 minutes.

7. Arrange skewers on platter. Serve with peanut sauce and cucumbers.

EACH SERVING CHICKEN: About 175 calories, 23g protein, 10g carbohydrate, 4g total fat (2g saturated), 60mg cholesterol, 350mg sodium

EACH 1 TABLESPOON PEANUT SAUCE: About 50 calories, 2g protein, 2g carbohydrate, 5g total fat (2g saturated), 0mg cholesterol, 90mg sodium

Grilled Buffalo Wings

Here's a crowd-pleaser. We made the tangy blue-cheese dipping sauce with reduced-fat mayonnaise, cutting calories but not the great taste.

PREP: 20 minutes   GRILL: 25 to 27 minutes
MAKES: 8 appetizer servings

BLUE-CHEESE DIPPING SAUCE

1   small container (8 ounces) sour cream (about 15 tablespoons)

4   ounces blue cheese, crumbled (about 1 cup)

¾   cup reduced-fat mayonnaise

1   green onion, finely chopped

2   tablespoons cider vinegar

1   teaspoon Worcestershire sauce

¼   teaspoon salt

BUFFALO WINGS

4   pounds medium chicken wings (about 24)

¾   cup cayenne pepper sauce (see Tip)

celery and carrot sticks

1. Prepare dipping sauce: In small bowl, with wire whisk, mix sour cream, blue cheese, mayonnaise, green onion, vinegar, Worcestershire sauce, and salt until well combined. Cover and refrigerate until ready to use or up to 3 days. Makes about 2 cups.

2. Prepare outdoor grill for covered direct grilling over medium heat.

3. Meanwhile, prepare wings: Separate wings at joints; refrigerate tips for another use. Place wings on hot grill rack over medium heat. Cover grill and cook wings, turning occasionally, until browned, about 20 minutes. Brush wings generously with cayenne pepper sauce and grill, brushing with remaining sauce and turning frequently, until glazed and juices run clear when thickest part of wing is pierced with tip of knife, 5 to 7 minutes longer.

4. Serve wings with dipping sauce and celery and carrot sticks.

EACH SERVING WINGS: About 300 calories, 27g protein, 1g carbohydrate, 20g total fat (6g saturated), 86mg cholesterol, 675mg sodium

EACH 1 TABLESPOON SAUCE: About 45 calories, 1g protein, 1g carbohydrate, 4g total fat (2g saturated), 8mg cholesterol, 105mg sodium

> **TIP:** Cayenne pepper sauce is a milder variety of hot pepper sauce that adds tang and flavor, not just heat. It can be found in the condiment section of the supermarket, near the ketchup.

Pesto and Mozzarella Pizzas

Garden tomatoes and basil make wonderful toppings for pizza cooked over the coals. Serve as a main course or cut into wedges for a fun appetizer.

PREP: 25 minutes   GRILL: about 4 minutes
MAKES: 4 pizzas or 4 main-dish servings

nonstick cooking spray

1   pound refrigerated fresh pizza dough from supermarket or pizzeria, at room temperature (see Tip, opposite)

¼   cup refrigerated pesto sauce

3   plum tomatoes, seeded and chopped

8   ounces fresh mozzarella cheese, thinly sliced

½   teaspoon coarsely ground black pepper

1. Prepare outdoor grill for covered direct grilling over medium heat.

2. Spray 2 large cookie sheets with cooking spray. On work surface, divide dough into quarters; spray with cooking spray. Press each piece of dough into a round about ⅛ inch thick. Transfer 2 rounds to each cookie sheet; cover loosely with plastic wrap. (Bring dough and topping ingredients to grill for pizza assembly.)

3. Place dough rounds on hot grill rack. Cover grill and cook until grill marks appear on underside and dough stiffens (dough may puff slightly), 2 to 3 minutes. With tongs, carefully return dough to cookie sheets, grilled side up.

4. Spread pesto on grilled side of dough rounds; top with tomatoes, mozzarella, and pepper.

5. Return pizzas to grill, toppings side up. Cover grill and cook until bottom of dough stiffens and mozzarella begins to melt, 2 to 3 minutes. Cut into wedges to serve.

EACH SERVING: About 530 calories, 19g protein, 59g carbohydrate, 24g total fat (9g saturated), 47mg cholesterol, 275mg sodium

MONTEREY JACK PIZZAS: Prepare recipe as in steps 1, 2, and 3. In step 4, spread *1 cup prepared black-bean dip* on grilled side of dough rounds; top with *1 cup shredded Monterey Jack or pepper jack cheese (4 ounces)*. Finish as in step 5. Transfer pizzas to board; top with *2 cups thinly sliced iceberg lettuce* and *½ cup of your favorite salsa*.

EACH SERVING MONTEREY JACK PIZZA: About 440 calories, 17g protein, 64g carbohydrate, 12g total fat (5g saturated), 25mg cholesterol, 1,080mg sodium

ARUGULA AND TOMATO PIZZAS: In cup, mix *1 tablespoon extra-virgin olive oil* and *1 tablespoon balsamic vinegar*. Prepare recipe as in steps 1, 2, and 3. In step 4, sprinkle *3 cups loosely packed baby arugula or spinach leaves* on grilled side of dough; top with *6 plum tomatoes (about 1 pound), thinly sliced*, and *2 ounces Parmesan cheese, thinly shaved with vegetable peeler (about ½ cup)*. Finish as in step 5. Transfer pizzas to cutting board; drizzle with balsamic mixture and sprinkle with *¼ teaspoon salt* and *⅛ teaspoon ground black pepper*.

EACH SERVING ARUGULA AND TOMATO PIZZA: About 400 calories, 15g protein, 60g carbohydrate, 12g total fat (4g saturated), 11mg cholesterol, 545mg sodium

Fontina and Pepper Pizza

Impress your guests with individual grilled pizzas topped with Fontina, roasted peppers, and a sprinkle of fresh marjoram.

PREP: 20 minutes   **GRILL:** 5 to 7 minutes
MAKES: 4 pizzas or 4 main-dish servings

1	pound refrigerated fresh pizza dough from supermarket or pizzeria, at room temperature (see Tip)
6	ounces Italian Fontina or Provolone cheese, shredded
2	jarred roasted red and/or yellow peppers, thinly sliced (1 cup)
1	tablespoon chopped fresh marjoram or thyme

1. Prepare outdoor grill for covered, direct grilling over medium-low heat.

2. Cut dough into 4 equal pieces. On one end of oiled cookie sheet, with fingertips, spread and flatten 1 piece of dough to about 1/8-inch thickness. (Edge does not need to be even.) On same cookie sheet, repeat with another piece of dough. Repeat with a second oiled cookie sheet and remaining dough.

3. Place all 4 pieces of dough, oiled side down, on hot grill rack. Cook until grill marks appear on underside (dough will stiffen and puff), 2 to 3 minutes.

4. With tongs, turn crusts over. Working quickly, arrange equal amounts Fontina and peppers on each crust. Cover grill and cook pizzas until undersides are evenly browned and cooked through, 3 to 4 minutes longer.

5. Transfer to cutting board; sprinkle with marjoram. Cut into wedges.

EACH SERVING: About 465 calories, 18g protein, 57g carbohydrate, 18g total fat (9g saturated), 49mg cholesterol, 640mg sodium

THREE-CHEESE PIZZA: Prepare pizza recipe as directed through step 3. In step 4, top crusts with *4 ounces fresh mozzarella cheese*, coarsely shredded; then dollop with *1/2 cup part-skim ricotta cheese*, and sprinkle with *1/3 cup freshly grated Pecorino Romano cheese* and *1/2 teaspoon coarsely ground black pepper*. In step 5, sprinkle *1 tablespoon chopped fresh parsley* over pizzas.

EACH SERVING THREE-CHEESE PIZZA: About 435 calories, 18g protein, 56g carbohydrate, 15g total fat (7g saturated), 38mg cholesterol, 260mg sodium

> **TIP:** Look for fresh pizza dough in the dairy section of your supermarket, usually near the tortillas. (Frozen pizza dough is also available. Allow several hours for it to thaw before using.) Or you can purchase dough from a local pizzeria; they'll usually sell it to you in 1-pound balls if you ask.

Tomato, Portobello, and Mozzarella Melts

To clean portobello mushrooms, wipe the caps with a damp paper towel to remove any dirt—never soak them in water.

PREP: **10 minutes**   GRILL: **7 to 10 minutes**
MAKES: **2 sandwiches or 4 servings**

2   cups loosely packed arugula or watercress, trimmed

2   tablespoons balsamic vinegar

1   loaf (about 1 inch thick) focaccia or ciabatta bread

4   large portobello mushrooms (about 1 pound total), stems removed and each cut in half

2   ripe medium tomatoes (6 to 8 ounces each), cut into ¾-inch-thick slices

2   tablespoons extra-virgin olive oil

¼   teaspoon salt

¼   teaspoon coarsely ground black pepper

4   ounces fresh mozzarella cheese, thinly sliced

1. Prepare outdoor grill for direct grilling over medium-high heat.

2. In small bowl, toss arugula and vinegar until evenly coated. From loaf of focaccia, with serrated knife, cut two 8″ by 2″ pieces. Cut each piece horizontally in half to make a total of four 8″ by 2″ pieces.

3. Brush mushrooms and tomatoes on both sides with oil; sprinkle with salt and pepper. Place mushrooms, stem-sides up, and tomatoes on hot grill rack and cook until tender and charred, 6 to 8 minutes, turning over once. Transfer tomatoes to plate. Arrange mozzarella on mushrooms; cover and cook until cheese melts, 1 to 2 minutes longer.

4. Place bread, cut-sides up, on work surface; top with arugula mixture, grilled tomatoes, and cheese-topped mushrooms. Cut each sandwich in half and serve immediately.

EACH SERVING: About 355 calories, 14g protein, 43g carbohydrate, 15g total fat (5g saturated), 22mg cholesterol, 595mg sodium

A KINDER CUT

Unless you have a razor-sharp edge on a chef's knife, you're better off using a serrated knife on a tomato, which will glide effortlessly through the skin and flesh instead of crushing it into a pulpy mess. Tip: To retain the juice inside the tomato, not on the cutting board, slice tomatoes from stem to blossom end instead of crosswise.

Croque Monsieur

A delicious take on a French classic.

PREP: 15 minutes   GRILL: 10 minutes
MAKES: 4 servings

2   tablespoons butter or margarine
1   tablespoon all-purpose flour
½   cup whole milk
salt and ground black pepper
ground nutmeg
8   slices firm white or country-style bread
2   ounces Gruyère, shredded (½ cup)
8   ounces sliced deli baked ham

1. In 1-quart saucepan, melt 1 tablespoon butter over medium heat. With wire whisk, stir in flour and cook until mixture browns slightly, 1 to 2 minutes, stirring constantly. Add milk and a pinch each of salt, pepper, and nutmeg. Heat to boiling, stirring 1 to 2 minutes longer or until sauce thickens. Remove from heat.

2. Spread remaining 1 tablespoon butter on one side of each slice of bread. Place 4 slices bread on work surface, buttered sides down; top with Gruyère. Arrange ham over cheese, folding slices to fit. Spread about 2 tablespoons sauce on 1 unbuttered side of each remaining bread slice. Top sandwiches with bread, sauce side down.

3. Heat large ridged grill pan on medium heat until hot. Arrange sandwiches in skillet with cheese layer on bottom. Cook sandwiches until bread is golden brown, about 6 minutes. Turn sandwiches over and cook until bread is brown and cheese melts, 3 to 4 minutes longer.

EACH SERVING: About 320 calories, 19g protein, 30g carbohydrate, 14g total fat (5g saturated), 47mg cholesterol, 1,115mg sodium

Grilled Three-Cheese Sandwiches

Upgrade the traditional pairing of a grilled-cheese sandwich and tomato soup and serve these outdoor-grilled sandwiches with a cold fresh tomato soup.

PREP: 10 minutes   GRILL: about 8 minutes
MAKES: 3 sandwiches or 6 servings

6   large slices sourdough bread,
      each about ½ inch thick
½   cup coarsely shredded Asiago cheese
6   ounces fresh mozzarella cheese, sliced
4   ounces Fontina cheese, sliced

1. Prepare outdoor grill for covered direct grilling over medium heat.

2. Place 3 slices bread on clean work surface. Sprinkle bread with Asiago, then top with mozzarella and Fontina. Top with remaining bread.

3. Place sandwiches on hot grill rack. Cover grill and cook until bread is toasted and cheese melts, 8 to 10 minutes, turning over once. Cut each sandwich in half to serve.

EACH SERVING: About 285 calories, 16g protein, 21g carbohydrate, 15g total fat (9g saturated), 49mg cholesterol, 525mg sodium

Peking Chicken Roll-Ups

The traditional Chinese recipe for duck is labor-intensive and takes several days to make. Our version, prepared in minutes, is made with grilled boneless chicken thighs and served in flour tortillas with hoisin sauce.

PREP: 25 minutes   **GRILL:** 10 to 12 minutes
MAKES: 4 servings

8	(8-inch) flour tortillas
2	tablespoons honey
2	tablespoons soy sauce
1	tablespoon grated, peeled fresh ginger
⅛	teaspoon ground red pepper (cayenne)
2	garlic cloves, crushed with garlic press
6	skinless, boneless chicken thighs (about 1¼ pounds total)
1	teaspoon vegetable oil
¼	cup hoisin sauce
½	English (seedless) cucumber, cut into 2 by ¼-inch matchsticks
2	green onions, thinly sliced

1. Prepare outdoor grill for direct grilling over medium-high heat.

2. Stack tortillas and wrap in foil. In small bowl, mix honey, soy sauce, ginger, ground red pepper, and garlic until blended. Set aside tortillas and honey mixture.

3. Coat chicken with oil and place on hot grill rack. Grill, turning once, 5 minutes. Brush chicken all over with honey mixture and grill until juices run clear when thickest part of thigh is pierced with tip of knife, 5 to 7 minutes longer, turning over once.

4. While chicken is cooking, place foil-wrapped tortillas on same grill rack and heat until warm, 3 to 5 minutes.

5. Transfer chicken to cutting board and thinly slice. Spread hoisin sauce on one side of tortillas. Top with chicken, cucumber, and green onions; roll up to serve.

EACH SERVING: About 400 calories, 27g protein, 50g carbohydrate, 10g total fat (3g saturated), 75mg cholesterol, 1,255mg sodium

Mediterranean Chicken Sandwiches

Kalamata olives, tomatoes, fennel seeds, and thyme give this sandwich its Mediterranean flavor profile. For double the grilled flavor, slice the bread as directed, then grill it alongside the chicken breasts for about 1 1/2 minutes per side.

PREP: 25 minutes   **GRILL:** 10 to 12 minutes

MAKES: 4 servings

1   teaspoon fennel seeds

1/2   teaspoon dried thyme

1/2   teaspoon salt

1/4   teaspoon coarsely ground black pepper

4   medium skinless, boneless chicken breast halves (about 1 1/4 pounds total)

1/4   cup Kalamata olives, pitted and minced

2   tablespoons mayonnaise

1   loaf (8 ounces) Italian bread

2   ripe small tomatoes (4 ounces each), each cut into 4 slices

1. Prepare outdoor grill for direct grilling over medium heat.

2. In mortar with pestle, crush fennel seeds with thyme, salt, and pepper. Rub both sides of chicken breasts with fennel-seed mixture; set aside.

3. In small bowl, mix olives and mayonnaise. Cut bread crosswise into 4 equal pieces, then cut each piece horizontally in half. Spread olive mixture evenly on cut sides of bread; set aside.

4. Place chicken on hot grill rack and grill until juices run clear when thickest part of breast is pierced with tip of knife, 10 to 12 minutes, turning over once. Transfer chicken to cutting board.

5. To assemble sandwiches, cut chicken breasts crosswise into 1/4-inch-thick slices. On bottom halves of bread, layer sliced chicken and tomatoes. Replace top halves of bread.

EACH SERVING: About 400 calories, 38g protein, 32g carbohydrate, 12g total fat (2g saturated), 86mg cholesterol, 910mg sodium

Grilled Green Tomato Focaccia Sandwiches

Instead of frying up green tomatoes, put slices on the grill for an elegant low-fat version of the Southern summer specialty. The smoke mellows yet brings out the tart taste of the not-quite-ripe tomato, balancing the salty Canadian bacon.

PREP: 20 minutes   **GRILL:** 11 to 13 minutes
MAKES: 4 servings

1	large lemon
½	cup light mayonnaise
½	teaspoon coarsely ground black pepper
3	medium (1 pound) green (unripe) tomatoes, cut into ½-inch-thick slices
¼	teaspoon salt
1	tablespoon olive oil
8	slices Canadian bacon
1	loaf focaccia bread, about 10" by 6" (1 pound), cut horizontally in half

1. Prepare outdoor grill for direct grilling over medium heat.

2. From lemon, grate 1 teaspoon peel and squeeze 2 tablespoons juice. In cup, combine lemon peel and juice, mayonnaise, and pepper.

3. Sprinkle tomato slices with salt; brush lightly with oil. Place tomatoes on hot grill rack and cook until browned and slightly softened, 6 to 7 minutes, turning over once. On same grill rack, cook Canadian bacon until heated through, 2 minutes, turning over once. Transfer tomatoes and bacon to platter. Place focaccia, cut sides down, on grill rack and grill until lightly toasted, 3 to 4 minutes.

4. Assemble sandwiches: Spread mayonnaise mixture on cut sides of focaccia. On bottom half of focaccia, layer tomatoes, then Canadian bacon. Replace top half of focaccia. To serve, cut sandwich into 4 pieces.

EACH SERVING: About 510 calories, 22g protein, 59g carbohydrate, 22g total fat (4g saturated), 40mg cholesterol, 1,565mg sodium

Backyard BLTs

Our piquant lemon-herb mayonnaise makes this classic sandwich even better than ever!

PREP: **15 minutes**   GRILL: **5 minutes**
MAKES: **4 servings**

1   lemon
⅓   cup light mayonnaise
1   tablespoon chopped fresh parsley
½   teaspoon chopped fresh thyme
⅛   teaspoon coarsely ground black pepper
3   ripe medium tomatoes (6 to 8 ounces each), cut into ¼-inch-thick slices
⅛   teaspoon salt
8   slices (½-inch-thick) sourdough bread
8   ounces thinly sliced Canadian bacon (about 24 slices)
8   small romaine lettuce leaves

1. Prepare outdoor grill for direct grilling over medium heat.

2. From lemon, grate ¼ teaspoon peel and squeeze 1 teaspoon juice. In small bowl, mix lemon peel and lemon juice with mayonnaise, parsley, thyme, and pepper until blended; set aside. Place tomato slices on sheet of waxed paper and sprinkle with salt.

3. With tongs, place bread slices on hot grill rack and grill just until grill marks appear on bottom side of bread. Set aside.

4. With tongs, place bacon slices on grill rack and grill just until grill marks appear on bacon, about 2 minutes (do not overcook; bacon will dry out and toughen).

5. To assemble sandwiches, spread mayonnaise mixture on ungrilled side of bread slices. Top 4 bread slices with half of bacon, all tomato, remaining bacon, then lettuce leaves. Place remaining 4 bread slices, grilled side up, on top. Cut each sandwich in half to serve.

EACH SERVING: About 315 calories, 17g protein, 32g carbohydrate, 14g total fat (2g saturated), 35mg cholesterol, 1,195mg sodium

Burgers

The burger is the bedrock of backyard grilling—what are Memorial Day, July 4th, and Labor Day without a grill full of sizzling burgers? We've got the recipe for The Perfect Burger, plus our "7 Secrets for a Great Burger," guaranteed to transform you into grillmeister extraordinaire. If you're looking for ideas to jazz up your basic beef burger, we've got you covered, with all sorts of fun twists, like Tex-Mex Burgers, Blue and Black Burgers, and BLT Burgers.

But how about striking out for territories beyond beef? We've included a delicious selection of pork, lamb, poultry, and fish burgers, including Greek Lamb Burgers with Minted Yogurt Sauce, Buffalo Chicken Burgers, and Grilled Cilantro Pork Burgers. And for those times when you'd like to go entirely meatless, try Portobello Mushroom Burgers or Bulgur Bean Burgers.

BLT Burgers, page 39

The Perfect Burger

One of the most important keys to a delicious, juicy burger is to handle the ground beef as little as possible. Shape your burgers without compacting them too much.

PREP: **10 minutes plus soaking skewers**
GRILL: **8 to 10 minutes**
MAKES: **4 burgers**

4   (12-inch) bamboo skewers

1¼   pounds ground beef chuck

½   teaspoon coarsely ground black pepper

1   teaspoon salt

1   large sweet onion (12 ounces), such as Vidalia or Maui, cut into ½-inch-thick rounds

4   hamburger buns, split

4   green-leaf lettuce leaves

2   ripe medium tomatoes (6 to 8 ounces each), thinly sliced

1. Soak skewers in *hot water* to cover at least 20 minutes. Meanwhile, prepare outdoor grill for covered direct grilling over medium heat, or preheat ridged grill pan over medium heat until very hot.

2. Shape ground beef into four ³/₄-inch-thick patties. Sprinkle pepper and ³/₄ teaspoon salt on both sides of patties. Thread 1 skewer through center of each onion slice. Sprinkle onion with remaining ¹/₄ teaspoon salt.

3. Place burgers and onion on hot grill; cook 8 to 10 minutes for medium or to desired doneness, turning over once. Onion should be browned and tender. About 1 minute before the burgers are done, add buns, cut sides down, to grill. Grill just until toasted. Serve burgers on buns with lettuce, tomato, and onion.

EACH BURGER: About 485 calories, 31g protein, 33g carbohydrate, 25g total fat (9g saturated), 96mg cholesterol, 920mg sodium

7 Secrets for a Great Burger

1. Ground chuck is a favorite for burgers. Its rich flavor is a perfect partner to just about any condiment you pair it with. Its juiciness is due to its fat content. Chuck is 81 to 85 percent lean. Be sure to get 1¼ pounds for 4 burgers, because 5 ounces raw cooks down to 4 ounces.

2. If not using meat right away, refrigerate it in its supermarket wrap for up to 2 days. (And don't let the meat or its juice touch other foods; the spread of *E. coli* and other bacteria is a real risk.) For longer storage, repackage it in freezer wrap or foil and freeze; use within 3 months.

3. Handle beef gently when shaping it, so you don't end up with a dense, dry burger. Start with a mound, flatten it slightly, and smooth around the edges.

4. Make sure the grill is hot before putting the burgers on. A hot grill sears the meat, so it won't stick.

5. Don't flatten patties with a spatula while grilling: Pressing squeezes out the flavorful juices and won't speed up cooking.

6. For safety's sake, cook thoroughly, until there's just a trace of pink in the center (medium doneness, 160°F). Burgers don't have to be well done to be safe to eat, just not rare. It's risky to eat undercooked burgers because bacteria on the surface of the meat before it's ground can be transferred to its interior during the grinding process. Cooking times vary, depending on the thickness of the burgers and the heat of the grill, so the only way to be sure they're done is to make them all the same size, then fork into one of them to check for doneness.

7. Cheese lovers, don't get more cheese on the grill slats than on the burgers. Once the patties are cooked to medium, blanket the top with Cheddar, Swiss, or another favorite, and cook with the grill lid down for about a minute.

Tex-Mex Burgers

For an all-out splurge, serve these burgers with shredded lettuce, sliced red onion, extra salsa, and a topping of guacamole. For a spicier burger, choose a medium to hot salsa and increase the chili powder to 2 teaspoons. You can also top the burger with sliced Monterey Jack. Just cover the grill to melt the cheese, and you've got a Tex-Mex cheeseburger.

PREP: 5 minutes   GRILL: 10 to 12 minutes
MAKES: 4 burgers

1   pound lean (90%) ground beef
2   tablespoons minced onion
2   tablespoons bottled salsa
½   teaspoon salt
1   teaspoon chili powder
4   seeded rolls, split

1. Prepare outdoor grill for direct grilling over medium heat, or lightly spray a ridged grill pan with nonstick cooking spray, then heat on medium until hot.

2. In medium bowl, combine ground beef, onion, salsa, salt, and chili powder just until well blended but not overmixed. Shape mixture into four ³/₄-inch-thick patties, each 1 inch thick, handling meat as gently as possible, for best texture.

3. Place burgers on hot grill rack or pan and grill, turning once, 10 to 12 minutes for medium or to desired doneness.

4. Place rolls, cut side down, on grill over medium heat and toast, without turning, just until grill marks appear on cut side of rolls. Serve burgers on rolls.

EACH BURGER: About 325 calories, 27g protein, 23g carbohydrate, 14g total fat (5g saturated), 70mg cholesterol, 670mg sodium

---

THE STEPS

1. Divide meat into 4 equal portions; shape each into a ³/₄-inch-thick patty. Handle as little as possible so burgers won't be tough.

2. Cook thoroughly.

BLT Burgers

Take a classic American sandwich and turn it into a burger—perfect. For photo, see page 34.

PREP: 15 minutes   GRILL: 10 to 12 minutes
MAKES: 4 burgers

¼   cup ketchup
¼   cup light mayonnaise
1   tablespoon yellow mustard
1¼ pounds ground beef chuck
8   slices bacon
4   sesame-seed buns, split
sliced sweet onion, tomato, and romaine
      lettuce leaves

1. Prepare outdoor grill for direct grilling over medium heat, or lightly spray a ridged grill pan with nonstick cooking spray, then heat on medium until hot.

2. In small bowl, stir ketchup, mayonnaise, and mustard until blended. Set aside. Makes about ½ cup.

3. Shape ground beef into four ¾-inch-thick burgers, handling beef as gently as possible. Wrap each with 2 strips bacon, perpendicular to each other.

4. Place burgers on hot grill rack or pan; cook 10 to 12 minutes for medium or desired doneness, turning over once.

5. During last 2 minutes of cooking burgers, place rolls, cut sides down, on grill rack and heat until lightly toasted. Serve burgers on buns with onion, tomato, lettuce, and sauce on the side.

EACH BURGER: About 575 calories, 34g protein, 27g carbohydrate, 36g total fat (12g saturated), 111mg cholesterol, 870mg sodium

Blue and Black Burgers

A rich blue cheese filling and a drizzle of basil olive oil set this gourmet burger apart.

PREP: 15 minutes   GRILL: 12 to 14 minutes
MAKES: 4 burgers

2   tablespoons olive oil
2   tablespoons chopped fresh basil
1¼ pounds ground beef chuck
4   ounces blue cheese, divided into four 1-inch
      chunks
¾   teaspoon salt
1   tablespoon coarsely ground black pepper
4   brioche rolls, split
4   thin slices sweet onion

1. Prepare outdoor grill for direct grilling over medium heat, or lightly spray a ridged grill pan with nonstick cooking spray, then heat on medium until hot. In cup, combine oil and basil; brush on 1 cut side of each roll. Set aside.

2. Hold one-fourth of beef in your hand; press a chunk of blue cheese into center, then lightly press meat around to enclose cheese. Burger will be about 1¼ inches thick. Repeat with remaining beef and blue cheese. Sprinkle burgers with salt and pepper to season both sides.

3. Place burgers on hot grill rack or pan; cook 12 to 14 minutes for medium or desired doneness, turning over once.

4. During last 2 minutes of cooking, place rolls, cut sides down, on grill rack and heat until lightly toasted. Serve burgers with rolls and onion.

EACH BURGER: About 745 calories, 40g protein, 39g carbohydrate, 47g total fat (17g saturated), 190mg cholesterol, 1,235mg sodium

Grilled Cilantro Pork Burgers

This is a wonderful Asian-style take on the pork burger—almost like a pork dumpling on a bun! You can also make these burgers using ground chicken or turkey.

PREP: **15 minutes**   GRILL: **10 to 12 minutes**

MAKES: **4 burgers**

¼ cup light mayonnaise

1 tablespoon soy sauce

1¼ pounds ground pork or chicken

½ cup loosely packed fresh cilantro leaves, coarsely chopped

3 green onions, chopped

1 tablespoon dry sherry

1 tablespoon finely chopped, peeled fresh ginger

1 teaspoon Asian sesame oil

¼ teaspoon crushed red pepper

¾ teaspoon salt

4 sesame-seed hamburger buns, split and toasted

1. Prepare outdoor grill for covered direct grilling over medium heat, or lightly spray a ridged grill pan with nonstick cooking spray, then heat on medium until hot.

2. In cup, stir mayonnaise and soy sauce until blended. Set aside.

3. In medium bowl, combine pork, cilantro, green onions, sherry, ginger, sesame oil, crushed red pepper, and salt until blended, but do not overmix. Shape pork mixture into four ¾-inch-thick burgers, handling meat gently for best texture.

4. Place burgers on hot grill rack or pan; cook until entirely cooked through, 10 to 12 minutes, turning over once—an instant-read meat thermometer inserted horizontally into center should register 160°F. (If using chicken or turkey, spray burgers with nonstick cooking spray and cook 12 to 14 minutes, to an internal temperature of 170°F.)

5. Serve burgers on buns with soy mayonnaise.

EACH BURGER: About 475 calories, 32g protein, 25g carbohydrate, 26g total fat (8g saturated), 106mg cholesterol, 1,120mg sodium

Greek Lamb Burgers with Minted Yogurt Sauce

These burgers can also be made with beef or poultry. If you decide to use chicken, spray the burgers with nonstick cooking spray and cook 12 to 14 minutes, to an internal temperature of 170°F.

PREP: **20 minutes**   GRILL: **10 TO 12 minutes**
MAKES: **4 burgers**

1   ripe plum tomato, chopped
½   cup plain low-fat yogurt
2   tablespoons light mayonnaise
¾   cup loosely packed fresh mint leaves, coarsely chopped
1   teaspoon salt
¼   teaspoon ground black pepper
1¼ pounds ground lamb
¼   cup walnuts, finely chopped (optional)
1   garlic clove, crushed with garlic press
2   teaspoons ground cumin
4   (6-inch) pitas
1   medium Kirby cucumber, sliced

1. Prepare outdoor grill for covered direct grilling over medium heat, or lightly spray a ridged grill pan with nonstick cooking spray, then heat on medium until hot.

2. In small bowl, stir tomato, yogurt, mayonnaise, 2 tablespoons mint, ¹/₄ teaspoon salt, and pepper until blended; set sauce aside. Makes about ³/₄ cup.

3. Prepare burgers: In medium bowl, combine lamb, walnuts, if using, garlic, cumin, ³/₄ teaspoon salt, and remaining mint until just blended. Shape lamb mixture into four ³/₄-inch-thick burgers, handling meat gently for best texture.

4. Place burgers on hot grill rack or pan; cook 10 to 12 minutes for medium or to desired doneness, turning over once. (An instant-read meat thermometer inserted horizontally into center should register 160°F.)

5. To serve, cut off one-third from side of each pita; save for another use. Place burgers in pitas with yogurt sauce and cucumber.

EACH BURGER: About 485 calories, 32g protein, 31g carbohydrate, 25g total fat (10g saturated), 105mg cholesterol, 985mg sodium

Your Basic Chicken Burger

Here's your chicken burger, straight up, plus three suggestions for jazzing it up.

PREP: 20 minutes   **GRILL:** 12 to 14 minutes
MAKES: 4 burgers

1   pound ground chicken breast
1   medium carrot, peeled and grated (½ cup)
2   green onions, finely chopped
1   garlic clove, crushed with garlic press
4   hamburger buns, split and toasted
sliced cucumber, lettuce leaves, and green onion (optional)

1. Prepare outdoor grill for direct grilling over medium heat, or lightly spray a ridged grill pan with nonstick cooking spray, then heat on medium until hot.

2. In medium bowl, combine ground chicken, carrot, green onions, and garlic (mixture will be very soft and moist). On waxed paper, shape mixture into four 3½-inch patties.

3. Place patties on hot grill rack or pan. If grill has widely spaced grates, place burgers on perforated grill topper to keep them intact. Grill, turning once, until juices run clear when center of burger is pierced with tip of knife, 12 to 14 minutes. (An instant-read thermometer inserted horizontally into center should register 170°F.)

4. Place burgers on buns. Serve with cucumber, lettuce, and green onions, if you like.

EACH BURGER: About 275 calories, 30g protein, 24g carbohydrate, 5g total fat (1g saturated), 72mg cholesterol, 310mg sodium

TERIYAKI CHICKEN BURGERS: Prepare basic burgers as directed, but add *2 tablespoons soy sauce, 1 tablespoon seasoned rice vinegar, 2 teaspoons grated, peeled fresh ginger*, and *2 teaspoons Asian sesame oil* to ground chicken mixture in step 2. (Prepare burger mixture just before cooking to prevent ginger from changing texture of meat.)

EACH TERIYAKI CHICKEN BURGER: About 305 calories, 31g protein, 26g carbohydrate, 8g total fat (2g saturated), 72mg cholesterol, 940mg sodium

BARBECUE CHICKEN BURGERS: Prepare basic burgers as directed, but add *2 tablespoons chili sauce, 1 tablespoon light (mild) molasses, 2 teaspoons cayenne pepper sauce, 2 teaspoons Worcestershire sauce*, and *¼ teaspoon salt* to ground chicken mixture in step 2.

EACH BARBECUE CHICKEN BURGER: About 295 calories, 31g protein, 30g carbohydrate, 5g total fat (1g saturated), 72mg cholesterol, 715mg sodium

HERB CHICKEN BURGERS: Prepare basic burgers as directed, but add *2 tablespoons finely chopped fresh dill, 1 tablespoon dried mint, 1 tablespoon fresh lemon juice, 1 teaspoon ground cumin, ½ teaspoon salt*, and *⅛ teaspoon ground red pepper (cayenne)* to ground chicken mixture in step 2.

EACH HERB CHICKEN BURGER: About 280 calories, 31g protein, 25g carbohydrate, 5g total fat (1g saturated), 72mg cholesterol, 605mg sodium

Buffalo Chicken Burgers

We paired the traditional Buffalo-wing flavors of pungent blue cheese and fiery hot sauce to create this exciting chicken burger.

PREP: 15 minutes   GRILL: 12 to 14 minutes
MAKES: 4 burgers

¼ cup light mayonnaise

¼ cup reduced-fat sour cream

2 ounces blue cheese, crumbled (about ½ cup)

2 teaspoons cider vinegar

½ teaspoon Worcestershire sauce

1¼ pounds ground chicken or turkey

1 stalk celery, finely chopped

3 tablespoons cayenne pepper sauce, plus more for serving

nonstick cooking spray

4 hamburger buns, split and toasted

lettuce leaves

carrot and celery sticks

1. Prepare outdoor grill for direct grilling over medium heat, or lightly spray a ridged grill pan with nonstick cooking spray, then heat on medium until hot.

2. In small bowl, stir mayonnaise, sour cream, blue cheese, vinegar, and Worcestershire until blended. Set blue cheese sauce aside. Makes about ³/₄ cup.

3. In medium bowl, combine chicken, celery, and cayenne pepper sauce just until blended. Shape mixture into four ³/₄-inch-thick burgers. Spray both sides of burgers with cooking spray.

4. Place burgers on hot grill rack or pan. If grill has widely spaced grates, place burgers on perforated grill topper to keep them intact. Grill, turning once, until juices run clear when center of burger is pierced with tip of knife, 12 to 14 minutes. (An instant-read meat thermometer inserted horizontally into center should register 170°F.)

5. Serve burgers on buns with lettuce and some blue cheese sauce. Serve remaining blue cheese sauce with carrot and celery sticks for dipping. Pass additional cayenne pepper sauce with burgers if you like.

EACH BURGER WITHOUT SAUCE: About 345 calories, 27g protein, 22g carbohydrate, 16g total fat (1g saturated), 0mg cholesterol, 785mg sodium

EACH 1 TABLESPOON BLUE CHEESE SAUCE: About 40 calories, 1g protein, 1g carbohydrate, 4g total fat (2g saturated), 7mg cholesterol, 110mg sodium

Asian Tuna Burgers

Finely chop the fish by hand for a light texture; using a food processor will make the patties dense and dry. Serve with or without a bun, with pickled ginger or Cucumber Relish (page 137).

PREP: **15 minutes**   GRILL: **6 to 7 minutes**
MAKES: **4 burgers**

1   tuna steak (about 1 pound)
1   green onion, thinly sliced
2   tablespoons reduced-sodium soy sauce
1   teaspoon grated, peeled fresh ginger
¼   teaspoon coarsely ground black pepper
¼   cup plain dried bread crumbs
2   tablespoons sesame seeds
nonstick cooking spray

1. Prepare outdoor grill for direct grilling over medium heat.

2. With large chef's knife, finely chop tuna and place in medium bowl. Add green onion, soy sauce, ginger, and pepper; mix until combined (mixture will be very soft and moist). Shape tuna mixture into four 3-inch round patties.

3. On waxed paper, combine bread crumbs and sesame seeds. Carefully press patties into mixture, turning to coat both sides. Spray both sides of tuna patties with cooking spray.

4. Place patties on hot grill rack and grill, turning once, until browned on the outside and still slightly pink in the center for medium-rare, 6 to 7 minutes, or to desired doneness.

EACH BURGER: About 210 calories, 26g protein, 7g carbohydrate, 8g total fat (2g saturated), 38mg cholesterol, 400mg sodium

Portobello Mushroom Burgers

Richly flavored, meaty-textured, portobellos are a satisfying substitute for real burgers— the swap saves you 16 grams fat, 76 milligrams cholesterol, and 200-plus calories.

PREP: **10 minutes**   GRILL: **10 to 11 minutes**
MAKES: **4 burgers**

2   packages (6 ounces each) portobello mushroom caps (4 large)
3   tablespoons bottled balsamic vinaigrette
⅓   cup light mayonnaise
¼   cup drained, jarred roasted red peppers
4   whole-wheat hamburger buns, split
1   large ripe tomato (10 to 12 ounces), thinly sliced
4   Boston lettuce leaves
2   large carrots, sliced diagonally

1. Heat ridged grill pan on medium-high until hot. Place mushrooms, stem sides down, in pan. Brush with half of vinaigrette and grill 5 minutes. Turn mushrooms over; brush with remaining vinaigrette and grill 5 to 6 minutes longer or until very tender.

2. Place mayonnaise and red pepper in blender. Pulse until peppers are chopped but not pureed, turning off blender and scraping down sides several times. Toast buns.

3. To serve, spread red pepper mayonnaise on bottom buns. Layer on mushrooms, tomato, lettuce, then bun tops. Serve with carrot slices.

EACH SERVING: About 270 calories, 8g protein, 33g carbohydrate, 12g total fat (2g saturated), 7mg cholesterol, 590mg sodium

Bulgur Bean Burgers

Satisfy vegetarians and meat eaters alike with these healthful, Middle Eastern–style burgers.

PREP: 20 minutes   **GRILL:** 15 minutes
MAKES: 4 burgers

1	cup water
3/4	teaspoon salt
1/2	cup bulgur
1	can (15 to 19 ounces) reduced-sodium black beans, rinsed and drained
1	container (6 ounces) plain low-fat yogurt
1/4	teaspoon ground allspice
1/4	teaspoon ground cinnamon
1/4	teaspoon ground cumin
1/4	cup loosely packed fresh mint leaves, finely chopped
	nonstick cooking spray
1	small Kirby cucumber, shredded
1/8	teaspoon ground black pepper
4	lettuce leaves
1	ripe medium tomato (6 to 8 ounces), sliced
4	whole-wheat hamburger buns, split

1. In 1-quart saucepan, heat water and 1/2 teaspoon salt to boiling over high heat. Stir in bulgur. Reduce heat to low; cover and simmer until water is absorbed, 12 to 14 minutes.

2. Meanwhile, in large bowl, with potato masher or fork, mash beans with 2 tablespoons yogurt until almost smooth. Stir in bulgur, allspice, cinnamon, cumin, and half of mint until combined. With lightly floured hands, shape bean mixture into four 3-inch round patties. (Patties can be made ahead. Cover and refrigerate up to 1 day.) Spray both sides of each patty lightly with cooking spray.

3. Heat ridged grill pan over medium heat until hot. Add burgers and cook until lightly browned and heated through, about 15 minutes, turning them over once.

4. While burgers are cooking, prepare yogurt sauce: In small bowl, combine cucumber, pepper, remaining yogurt, remaining mint, and remaining 1/4 teaspoon salt. Makes about 1 1/4 cups.

5. To serve, divide lettuce, tomato slices, and burgers among buns; top with some yogurt sauce. Serve with remaining yogurt sauce on the side.

EACH BURGER: About 295 calories, 16g protein, 58g carbohydrate, 3g total fat (1g saturated), 3mg cholesterol, 960mg sodium

Poultry

Poultry can pose a challenge to some cooks. How do you make sure it's cooked all the way through without incinerating it? Follow our easy directions and we guarantee your days of burned on the outside but raw on the inside will be over. We've also included a chart of approximate cook times for different chicken parts (legs, thighs, etc.), as well as the internal temperature they should be cooked to, and our strategies for cooking chicken safely.

Whether you want to grill your chicken whole or cut it into kabobs, we've got a toothsome collection of recipes to pick from. We've also included recipes that are tailor made to serve at a party, like Ginger-Grilled Chicken for a Crowd and Sweet and Tangy BBQ Chicken, where the chicken is oven-steamed in advance. And don't forget turkey—you can spice it, wrap it, or add herbs for a flavorful change of pace from chicken.

Lemon-Mint Chicken Cutlets on Watercress, page 57

Ginger-Grilled Chicken for a Crowd

When you have a crowd to feed at a backyard bash, try this honey-and-ginger party pleaser.

PREP: **10 minutes** plus overnight to marinate
GRILL: **30 to 35 minutes**

MAKES: **12 main-dish servings**

1¼ cups soy sauce

¾ cup honey

¼ cup fresh lemon juice (about 2 large lemons)

2 tablespoons vegetable oil

2 tablespoons minced, peeled fresh ginger

2 garlic cloves, crushed with garlic press

3 chickens (3 pounds each), each cut into quarters

1. In small bowl, combine soy sauce, honey, lemon juice, oil, ginger, and garlic until well blended. Divide chicken and marinade among three zip-tight plastic bags, turning chicken to coat; place in 15″ by 9″ baking dish. Seal bags, pressing out as much air as possible. Refrigerate overnight to marinate.

2. Prepare outdoor grill for covered direct grilling over medium heat.

3. Remove chicken from marinade; discard marinade. Place chicken on grill, cover, and cook until golden brown, about 5 minutes per side. Move chicken to perimeter of grill (where it is cooler); cover and cook until juices run clear when thickest part of chicken is pierced with tip of knife, 20 to 25 minutes longer.

EACH SERVING: About 410 calories, 42g protein, 10g carbohydrate, 22g total fat (6g saturated), 132mg cholesterol, 988mg sodium

---

GRILLING CHICKEN

Different chicken parts require different amounts of time to cook, but it is nice to be able to remove all the chicken from the grill at the same time so it is equally hot. Here's an easy way to accomplish this: When grilling a cut-up chicken, put the legs on first. After 5 minutes, place the breast on the grill. After another 10 minutes, put the thighs on the grill to cook.

CUT	COOK-TO INTERNAL TEMPERATURE	APPROXIMATE COOK TIME
Legs, bone-in	170°F	30–35 minutes
Thighs, bone-in	170°F	12–15 minutes
Thighs, boneless	170°F	10–12 minutes
Breasts, bone-in	165°F	25–30 minutes
Breasts, boneless	160°F	10–12 minutes
Whole chicken (about 3½ pounds)	170°F	1 hour to 1 hour 15 minutes

Beer-Can Chicken

Your favorite brew keeps this chicken moist and juicy. If using a charcoal grill, you will need to add ten fresh charcoal briquettes per side if more than an hour of cooking is required.

PREP: 15 minutes plus standing
GRILL: 1 hour to 1 hour 15 minutes
MAKES: 8 main-dish servings

3	tablespoons paprika
1	tablespoon sugar
1	tablespoon salt
2	teaspoons coarsely ground black pepper
1	teaspoon onion powder
1	teaspoon garlic powder
1	teaspoon ground red pepper (cayenne)
2	chickens (about 3½ pounds each)
2	cans beer (12 ounces each)

1. Prepare charcoal fire for covered indirect-heat grilling with drip pan as manufacturer directs or preheat gas grill for covered indirect grilling over medium heat.

2. In small bowl, combine paprika, sugar, salt, black pepper, onion powder, garlic powder, and ground red pepper.

3. Remove giblets and necks from chickens. Rinse chickens with cold running water; drain well and pat dry with paper towels. Sprinkle 1 tablespoon spice mixture inside cavity of each chicken. Rub remaining spice mixture all over chickens.

4. Wipe beer cans clean. Open beer cans; pour off ½ cup beer from each can and reserve for another use. With can opener (church key), make four more holes in top of each can. Place 1 partially filled beer can on flat surface; hold 1 chicken upright, with opening of body cavity down, and slide chicken over top of can so can fits inside cavity. Repeat with remaining chicken and can. Carefully set chickens over drip pan or away from the heat source on a gas grill. Spread out legs to balance chickens on rack. Cover grill and cook chickens until juices run clear when thickest part of thigh is pierced with tip of knife, 1 hour to 1 hour 15 minutes.

5. With tongs and barbecue mitts, carefully remove chickens and cans from grill, being careful not to spill beer. Let chicken stand 10 minutes before lifting from cans. Transfer chickens to large platter or carving board; discard beer. Cut each chicken into 8 serving pieces.

EACH SERVING: About 350 calories, 39g protein, 4g carbohydrate, 19g total fat (5g saturated), 152mg cholesterol, 985mg sodium

Sweet and Tangy BBQ Chicken

It wouldn't be an American summer get-together without grilled chicken brushed with our delicious homemade barbecue sauce. To help you enjoy more time with your guests and not worry about undercooking, completely precook the chicken in the oven and keep it refrigerated up to a day. Then, when you're ready to dine, just warm up the chicken on the grill and brush on the sauce.

PREP: 15 minutes plus oven-steaming
GRILL: 15 to 20 minutes
MAKES: 12 main-dish servings

OVEN-STEAMED CHICKEN

3   chickens (about 4 pounds each), each cut into quarters, skin removed if you like

1½ teaspoons salt

2   lemons, cut into wedges

1   large onion (12 ounces), cut into wedges

SWEET AND TANGY BARBECUE SAUCE

1   tablespoon olive oil

1   large onion (12 ounces), chopped

3   garlic cloves, crushed with garlic press

¼   cup chili powder

1   can (28 ounces) tomato puree

1   jar (12 ounces) apricot preserves

½   cup cider vinegar

3   tablespoons spicy brown mustard

2   tablespoons Worcestershire sauce

1   teaspoon salt

1. Prepare oven-steamed chicken: Preheat oven to 425°F. Arrange chicken quarters in large roasting pan (17″ by 11½″), overlapping pieces if necessary. Sprinkle chicken with salt; top with lemon wedges and onion. Cover roast-ing pan tightly with heavy-duty foil. Oven-steam chicken until juices run clear when thickest part of chicken is pierced with tip of knife, about 1¼ hours, turning chicken halfway through baking time to ensure even cooking. Discard lemons and onion. Refrigerate broth for use another day. Transfer chicken to large platter; cover and refrigerate until ready to grill.

2. Prepare barbecue sauce: In 5- to 6-quart saucepot, heat oil over medium heat until hot. (Do not use a smaller pan; sauce bubbles up and splatters during cooking—the deeper the pan, the better.) Add chopped onion and cook until tender and golden, about 10 minutes, stirring occasionally. Add garlic and chili powder; cook 1 minute. Remove saucepot from heat; carefully stir in remaining sauce ingredients. Heat sauce to boiling over medium-low heat and cook, par-tially covered, 10 minutes to thicken slightly, stirring occasionally.

3. Transfer sauce to bowl; if not using right away, cover and store up to 1 week in refrigerator or 2 months in freezer. Makes about 6 cups.

4. Prepare outdoor grill for covered direct grill-ing over medium heat. Reserve 3 cups barbecue sauce for serving. Place chicken on hot grill rack; cover grill and cook 10 minutes, turning chicken once. Cook chicken 5 to 10 minutes longer, turn-ing occasionally and frequently brushing with remaining sauce until chicken is heated through and sauce is browned. Heat reserved sauce to serve with chicken.

EACH SERVING: About 315 calories, 44g protein, 6g carbohydrate, 12g total fat (3g saturated), 135mg cholesterol, 540mg sodium

Grilled Bone-In Chicken Breasts, Three Ways

This simple recipe for grilled chicken breasts on the bone with crisp skin and juicy meat takes on a new dimension when one of our flavorful mixtures is rubbed under the skin: Sun-Dried Tomato and Basil, Garlic-Herb, or Sage-Butter.

PREP: **15 minutes**   GRILL: **about 25 minutes**

MAKES: **4 main-dish servings**

choice of seasoning mixture (right)
2   whole bone-in chicken breasts, split (about 2½ pounds total)
½   teaspoon salt
¼   teaspoon coarsely ground black pepper

1. Prepare outdoor grill for direct grilling over medium heat.

2. Prepare one seasoning mixture as directed.

3. With fingertips, separate skin from meat on each breast half. Rub equal amounts of seasoning mixture under skin of each breast. Sprinkle chicken with salt and pepper.

4. Place chicken on hot grill rack and grill, turning over once, until juices run clear when thickest part of breast is pierced with tip of knife, about 25 minutes.

SUN-DRIED TOMATO AND BASIL SEASONING: In small bowl, mix *2 sun-dried tomatoes packed in seasoned olive oil*, minced, and *¼ cup loosely packed fresh basil leaves*, finely chopped.

EACH SERVING SUN-DRIED TOMATO AND BASIL CHICKEN: About 305 calories, 46g protein, 0g carbohydrate, 12g total fat (3g saturated), 129mg cholesterol, 405mg sodium

GARLIC-HERB SEASONING: In small bowl, mix *2 garlic cloves*, crushed with garlic press; *1 tablespoon chopped fresh rosemary leaves*; *1 tablespoon olive oil*; and *1 teaspoon freshly grated lemon peel.*

EACH SERVING GARLIC-HERB CHICKEN: About 335 calories, 46g protein, 1g carbohydrate, 15g total fat (4g saturated), 129mg cholesterol, 400mg sodium

SAGE-BUTTER SEASONING: In small bowl, mix *1 tablespoon softened butter or margarine* and *1 tablespoon chopped fresh sage.*

EACH SERVING SAGE-BUTTER CHICKEN: About 330 calories, 46g protein, 0g carbohydrate, 15g total fat (5g saturated), 137mg cholesterol, 417mg sodium

Lemon Chicken with Grilled Summer Squash

For this easy summer supper, simply toss the sliced squash on the grill along with the marinated chicken. You can use zucchini, yellow squash, or a combination.

PREP: 15 minutes plus marinating
GRILL: 10 to 12 minutes
MAKES: 4 main-dish servings

1	large lemon
1	tablespoon olive oil
½	teaspoon salt
¼	teaspoon coarsely ground black pepper
4	medium skinless, boneless chicken thighs (about 1¼ pounds)
4	medium yellow summer squash and/or zucchini (about 6 ounces each), each cut lengthwise into 4 wedges
¼	cup snipped fresh chives

1. From lemon, grate 1 tablespoon peel and squeeze 3 tablespoons juice. In medium bowl, whisk together lemon peel and juice, oil, salt, and pepper; transfer 2 tablespoons marinade to cup and reserve.

2. Add chicken to bowl with marinade; toss until evenly coated. Cover and let stand 15 minutes at room temperature or 30 minutes in the refrigerator.

3. Meanwhile, prepare outdoor grill for covered direct grilling over medium heat.

4. Discard chicken marinade. Place chicken and squash on hot grill rack. Cover grill and cook, turning chicken and squash over once and removing pieces as they are done, until juices run clear when thickest part of thigh is pierced with tip of knife and squash is tender and browned, 10 to 12 minutes.

5. Transfer chicken and squash to cutting board. Cut chicken into 1-inch-wide strips; cut each squash wedge crosswise in half.

6. To serve, on large platter, toss squash with reserved lemon-juice marinade, then toss with chicken and sprinkle with chives.

EACH SERVING: About 255 calories, 29g protein, 8g carbohydrate, 8g total fat (3g saturated), 101mg cholesterol, 240mg sodium

Grilled Chicken Quarters with Grape Tomato Salad

To mellow the strong flavor and take the bite out of a raw onion, we like to soak it, sliced or chopped, in ice water for 10 minutes—or a little longer for an even sweeter flavor.

PREP: 25 minutes   GRILL: 30 to 40 minutes
MAKES: 4 main-dish servings

4 to 5 lemons

3   garlic cloves, crushed with garlic press

1   teaspoon olive oil

1¼ teaspoons kosher salt

¾   teaspoon coarsely ground black pepper

1   chicken (about 4 pounds), cut into quarters (see Tip, right)

¼   cup finely chopped red onion

¼   cup loosely packed fresh basil leaves, chopped

2   pints (about 4 cups) grape or cherry tomatoes, each cut in half

1. Prepare outdoor grill for covered direct grilling over medium heat.

2. From 3 to 4 lemons, grate 3 tablespoons plus 1 teaspoon peel and squeeze 1 tablespoon juice. Cut remaining lemon into 4 wedges and reserve for serving with chicken.

3. In small bowl, combine 3 tablespoons lemon peel with garlic, oil, 1 teaspoon salt, and ½ teaspoon pepper. With fingertips, gently separate chicken skin from meat on chicken breasts and thighs. Rub half of lemon-peel mixture on meat under skin; rub remaining mixture all over skin.

4. Place chicken on hot grill rack. Cover grill and cook chicken until juices run clear when thickest part of thigh is pierced with tip of knife, 30 to 40 minutes, turning over once. Transfer chicken pieces to platter as they are done.

5. Meanwhile, place chopped onion in *cup of ice water* and soak 10 minutes; drain well. In medium bowl, combine onion, basil, tomato halves, lemon juice, and remaining ¼ teaspoon salt, ¼ teaspoon pepper, and 1 teaspoon lemon peel. Makes about 4 cups.

6. Arrange each chicken quarter on a dinner plate and top with grape tomato salad. Garnish each plate with a reserved lemon wedge.

EACH SERVING: About 455 calories, 47g protein, 11g carbohydrate, 24g total fat (7g saturated), 182mg cholesterol, 755mg sodium

---

TIP: To deliver this irresistible dish to the dinner table even faster, replace the chicken quarters with 1½ pounds turkey cutlets or thin-sliced chicken cutlets. Proceed as above, but reduce grilling time to 5 to 7 minutes, turning cutlets over once.

A Guide to Grilling Chicken

GREASE YOUR GRILL: Chances are you won't have a sticking problem if your chicken has skin, or if it's marinated or rubbed with some oil. But play it safe. Before you light the grill, spray the rack with nonstick cooking spray or brush it with oil.

KEEP IT HOT: Sear the chicken on a hot grill—this makes it easier to turn the chicken over.

WATCH SEASONINGS CAREFULLY: Marinades and basting sauces, many of which have a high sugar content, will burn if the grill temperature is too hot or if exposed to heat for too long. A hot grill is normally not a problem with quick-cooking chicken cuts (such as skinless, boneless breasts), but longer-cooking cuts (such as bone-in chicken parts) should be cooked over a lower heat. And don't start basting until the chicken is almost fully cooked.

CLOSE THE TOP: If your grill has a cover, cook bone-in chicken with the cover down. It will make your grill more ovenlike, and your food will cook more evenly. Also, because the cover cuts off some of the oxygen, you'll have fewer flare-ups.

BE PATIENT: Resist the urge to continuously move the poultry around while it cooks. The chicken will cook more evenly (and more quickly!) if you follow the recipe cooking instructions or turn it over only once midway through grilling.

USE THE RIGHT UTENSIL: Use long-handled tongs or a wide metal spatula to move the chicken. Poking it with a fork will allow precious juices to escape.

TEST FOR DONENESS: Don't risk serving undercooked chicken. When in doubt, make a small cut into the thickest part so you can be positive that it's no longer pink inside. You can also use an instant-read meat thermometer to see if your meat has reached a safe internal temperature, 170°F for whole chicken and 160°F for breasts.

BE SURE TO CLEAN UP: Scrape your grill rack after each use; otherwise, the chicken will pick up charred bits from your last barbecue. Chicken has a tendency to stick to a dirty grill.

Chicken with Gremolata Salsa

Gremolata, a sprightly combination of parsley, lemon peel, and garlic, is tossed with sun-ripened tomatoes for a full-flavored summer treat. For a change, try grated orange peel instead of the lemon, and basil instead of the parsley. If you like, remove the skin from the chicken and brush the quarters with a tablespoon of oil before cooking to lighten the dish.

PREP: 15 minutes   GRILL: 40 to 45 minutes
MAKES: 4 main-dish servings

4	ripe medium tomatoes (6 to 8 ounces each), cut into ¼-inch pieces
2	tablespoons finely chopped fresh parsley
1	teaspoon freshly grated lemon peel
1	small garlic clove, minced
1	teaspoon olive oil
1	teaspoon salt
½	teaspoon coarsely ground black pepper
1	chicken (about 3½ pounds), cut into quarters

1. Prepare outdoor grill for direct grilling over medium heat.

2. In small bowl, stir tomatoes, parsley, lemon peel, garlic, oil, ¹/₂ teaspoon salt, and ¹/₄ teaspoon pepper; set salsa aside. Makes about 3 cups.

3. Sprinkle chicken with remaining ¹/₂ teaspoon salt and ¹/₄ teaspoon pepper.

4. Place chicken on hot grill rack and grill 20 minutes. Turn over and grill until juices run clear when thickest part of chicken is pierced with tip of knife, 20 to 25 minutes longer.

5. Serve chicken with salsa.

EACH SERVING: About 460 calories, 49g protein, 6g carbohydrate, 25g total fat (7g saturated), 154mg cholesterol, 740mg sodium

> **TIP:** Mix up a batch of this lemon-scented tomato salsa to spoon over grilled zucchini, eggplant, or a mixture of vegetables.

Lemon-Mint Chicken Cutlets on Watercress

The tang of lemon and the peppery punch of watercress make this a refreshing choice on a hot summer night. Another plus is that these thin cutlets will cook up in just a few minutes. For photo, see page 46.

PREP: 15 minutes   GRILL: 4 to 5 minutes

MAKES: 4 main-dish servings

1¼   pounds thinly sliced skinless, boneless chicken breasts

2   lemons

2   tablespoons olive oil

2   tablespoons chopped fresh mint, plus more for garnish

½   teaspoon salt

½   teaspoon coarsely ground black pepper

1   bag (4 ounces) baby watercress

1. Heat ridged grill pan over medium-high heat (or prepare outdoor grill for direct grilling over medium-high heat).

2. Pound chicken to uniform ¼-inch thickness if necessary (see below).

3. From lemons, grate 1 tablespoon plus 1½ teaspoons peel and squeeze 3 tablespoons juice. In large bowl, mix lemon peel and juice, oil, 2 tablespoons mint, salt, and pepper until dressing is blended.

4. Reserve ¼ cup dressing. In large bowl, toss chicken cutlets with remaining dressing. Place chicken in grill pan and cook until juices run clear when breast is pierced with tip of knife, 4 to 5 minutes, turning over once.

5. To serve, toss watercress with reserved dressing and top with chicken. Sprinkle with additional chopped mint for garnish.

EACH SERVING: About 225 calories, 34g protein, 2g carbohydrate, 9g total fat (1g saturated), 82mg cholesterol, 375mg sodium

---

THE GENTLE ART OF POUNDING

Here's how to pound a chicken breast to a uniform thickness.

1. Place a skinless, boneless chicken breast half between 2 sheets of plastic wrap and place on a cutting board or work surface. The plastic wrap will protect the surface of the chicken and prevent the meat from sticking to the mallet and the cutting board—and it won't rip as easily as waxed paper. The same 2 sheets of plastic wrap can be reused for remaining chicken breasts.

2. Use the smooth side of a metal or wood meat mallet. (The textured side is good for tough cuts of meat that need to be tenderized.) If you don't have a meat mallet, you can use a sturdy rolling pin or the flat side of a heavy skillet. Gently strike the chicken breast until it has an even thickness, ⅛ to ¼ inch thick, depending on the recipe. It's not necessary to strike the breast with a great deal of force; let the mallet do the work!

Curried Chicken with Mango-Cantaloupe Slaw

Here, curry, crystallized ginger, and crushed red pepper bring out the flavor of the fresh fruit.

PREP: 25 minutes plus marinating
GRILL: 10 to 12 minutes
MAKES: 4 main-dish servings

1 to 3 limes

1   small container (6 ounces) plain low-fat yogurt

¾   teaspoon curry powder

4   tablespoons chopped crystallized ginger

1   teaspoon salt

¼   teaspoon crushed red pepper

4   medium skinless, boneless chicken breast halves (about 1¼ pounds total)

½   small cantaloupe, rind removed, seeded and cut into julienne strips (2 cups)

1   large mango, peeled and cut into julienne strips (2 cups)

½   cup loosely packed fresh cilantro leaves, chopped

1   head Boston lettuce

1. Grease grill rack. Prepare outdoor grill for direct grilling over medium heat, or lightly spray a ridged grill pan with nonstick cooking spray, then heat on medium until hot.

2. From 1 or 2 limes, grate ½ teaspoon peel and squeeze 2 tablespoons juice. In large bowl, combine 1 tablespoon lime juice and ¼ teaspoon lime peel with yogurt, curry powder, 2 tablespoons ginger, ¾ teaspoon salt, and ⅛ teaspoon crushed red pepper; whisk until blended. Add chicken, turning to coat. Cover and let stand 15 minutes at room temperature or 30 minutes in refrigerator, turning occasionally.

3. Meanwhile, in medium bowl, with rubber spatula, gently stir cantaloupe and mango with cilantro, remaining 2 tablespoons ginger, 1 tablespoon lime juice, ¼ teaspoon lime peel, ¼ teaspoon salt, and ⅛ teaspoon crushed red pepper; set slaw aside. Makes about 4 cups.

4. Remove chicken from marinade; discard marinade. Place chicken on hot grill rack or pan. Cover and cook until juices run clear when thickest part of breast is pierced with tip of knife, 10 to 12 minutes, turning over once. Transfer chicken to cutting board; cool slightly to allow juices to set for easier slicing, then cut into long, thin slices.

5. To serve, divide lettuce leaves among 4 dinner plates; top with chicken and slaw. If you like, cut remaining lime into wedges and use for garnish.

EACH SERVING WITH LETTUCE: About 205 calories, 34g protein, 5g carbohydrate, 4g total fat (1g saturated), 92mg cholesterol, 330mg sodium

EACH ½ CUP SLAW: About 50 calories, 1g protein, 13g carbohydrate, 0g total fat, 0mg cholesterol, 150mg sodium

Indian-Style Chicken with Grilled Mango Chutney

If you've ever tried to cut a mango and mangled the flesh, ending up with a mushy mess, check out the GHRI-tested OXO Good Grips mango splitter. It easily cuts through a firm-ripe mango, separating the seed from the flesh.

PREP: 20 minutes plus marinating
GRILL: 28 to 33 minutes

MAKES: 4 main-dish servings

3   tablespoons plain low-fat yogurt
1   tablespoon paprika
1½   teaspoons ground cumin
1½   teaspoons ground coriander
½   teaspoon ground red pepper (cayenne)
1   garlic clove, crushed with garlic press
4½   teaspoons grated, peeled fresh ginger
¾   teaspoon salt
4   medium bone-in chicken breast halves (about 2 pounds total), skin removed
2   firm, ripe mangoes
1   tablespoon light brown sugar
1   tablespoon cider vinegar
1   small green onion, thinly sliced
cooked basmati rice (optional)

1. In small bowl, mix yogurt, paprika, cumin, coriander, red pepper, garlic, 4 teaspoons ginger, and ½ teaspoon salt until blended. Pour yogurt marinade into large zip-tight plastic bag; add chicken, turning to coat. Seal bag, pressing out excess air. Place on plate and refrigerate at least 1 hour or up to 4 hours.

2. Prepare outdoor grill for covered direct grilling over medium heat.

3. Peel mangoes and cut lengthwise; slice from each side of long, flat seed, as close to seed as possible. Cut away remaining flesh from around seed in as few pieces as possible. Place mango on hot grill rack and cook until lightly charred and tender, about 8 minutes, turning over halfway through grilling. Transfer mangoes to cutting board and set aside until cool enough to handle.

4. Coarsely chop grilled mangoes and place in medium bowl. Add brown sugar, vinegar, green onion, remaining ¼ teaspoon salt, and remaining ½ teaspoon ginger; stir to combine. Makes about 2 cups.

5. Remove chicken from marinade; discard marinade. Place chicken on hot grill rack. Cover grill and cook until juices run clear when thickest part of breast is pierced with tip of knife, 20 to 25 minutes, turning over once. Place on platter and serve with mango chutney and, if you like, basmati rice.

EACH SERVING CHICKEN: About 170 calories, 35g protein, 2g carbohydrate, 2g total fat (1g saturated), 85mg cholesterol, 375mg sodium

EACH ¼ CUP CHUTNEY: About 40 calories, 0g protein, 11g carbohydrate, 1g total fat (0g saturated), 0mg cholesterol, 75mg sodium

Grilled Boneless Chicken Breasts with a Trio of Sauces

It's easy to grill chicken breasts a day or two ahead, so they are perfect party fare. Serve cold or at room temperature with sauce of choice.

PREP: **10 minutes**   GRILL: **10 to 12 minutes**
MAKES: **16 main-dish servings**

16   medium skinless, boneless chicken-breast halves (about 5 pounds total)
2   tablespoons olive oil
2   teaspoons freshly grated lemon peel
1   teaspoon salt
½   teaspoon coarsely ground black pepper
lemon leaves for garnish
Peach Salsa, Walnut Sauce, and/or Parsley-Caper Sauce (right)

1. Prepare outdoor grill for direct grilling over medium heat, or lightly spray a ridged grill pan with nonstick cooking spray, then heat on medium until hot.

2. In large bowl, toss chicken breasts with oil, lemon peel, salt, and pepper until evenly coated.

3. Place chicken on hot grill rack or pan (in batches if necessary) and cook until juices run clear when thickest part of breast is pierced with tip of knife, 10 to 12 minutes, turning over once. Transfer chicken to platter; cover and refrigerate up to 2 days if not serving right away.

4. To serve, garnish platter with lemon leaves. Provide sauces on the side.

EACH SERVING CHICKEN: About 190 calories, 33g protein, 0g carbohydrate, 6g total fat (1g saturated), 90mg cholesterol, 225mg sodium

PEACH SALSA: Stir *3 pounds ripe peaches*, peeled, pitted, and cut into ½-inch cubes; *1 green onion*, finely chopped; *2 tablespoons fresh lime juice; 1 small hot red pepper*, seeded and minced, and *½ teaspoon salt* until mixed. Refrigerate up to 4 hours. Makes 4 cups.

EACH ¼ CUP PEACH SALSA: About 30 calories, 1g protein, 7g carbohydrate, 0g total fat, 0mg cholesterol, 75mg sodium

WALNUT SAUCE: In food processor, blend *2 cups walnuts*, toasted; *1 garlic clove*; and *3 slices firm white bread*, torn into large pieces until finely ground. Add *1 cup reduced-sodium chicken broth, ⅓ cup reduced-fat sour cream, ¾ teaspoon salt, ½ teaspoon sweet paprika,* and *⅛ teaspoon ground red pepper (cayenne)* and blend until combined. Refrigerate up to 3 days. Sprinkle with *paprika* for garnish. Makes 2½ cups.

EACH TABLESPOON WALNUT SAUCE: About 45 calories, 1g protein, 2g carbohydrate, 4g total fat (1g saturated), 1g cholesterol, 70mg sodium

PARSLEY-CAPER SAUCE: In food processor, blend together *3 cups loosely packed fresh parsley leaves, ⅓ cup olive oil, ¼ cup drained capers, ⅛ teaspoon ground red pepper (cayenne), 1 garlic clove*, and *4 teaspoons water* until very finely chopped. Refrigerate up to 2 days. Makes 1 cup.

EACH 2 TABLESPOONS PARSLEY-CAPER SAUCE: About 45 calories, 0g protein, 1g carbohydrate, 5g total fat (1g saturated), 0mg cholesterol, 70mg sodium

Grilled Chicken Breasts with Tomato-Olive Relish

Our tasty no-cook relish was inspired by Italian puttanesca sauce. Serve with a crisp green vegetable or a Mediterranean side dish like Grilled Eggplant with Feta and Fresh Mint (page 130).

PREP: 15 minutes   GRILL: 10 to 12 minutes
MAKES: 4 main-dish servings

2   ripe medium tomatoes (6 to 8 ounces each), cut into ¼-inch pieces

¼   cup Kalamata olives, pitted and coarsely chopped, plus whole olives for garnish

2   tablespoons minced red onion

2   tablespoons capers, drained

1   teaspoon red wine vinegar

3   teaspoons olive oil

4   small skinless, boneless chicken breast halves (about 1 pound total)

¼   teaspoon salt

¼   teaspoon coarsely ground black pepper

1. In small bowl, mix tomatoes, olives, onion, capers, vinegar, and 1 teaspoon oil; set aside.

2. Prepare outdoor grill for direct grilling over medium heat, or lightly spray a ridged grill pan with nonstick cooking spray, then heat on medium until hot.

3. In medium bowl, toss chicken with salt, pepper, and remaining 2 teaspoons oil until evenly coated.

4. Place chicken on hot grill rack or pan and grill until juices run clear when thickest part of breast is pierced with tip of knife, 10 to 12 minutes, turning over once.

5. To serve, top chicken with tomato-olive relish and garnish with olives.

EACH SERVING: About 200 calories, 27g protein, 5g carbohydrate, 7g total fat (1g saturated), 66mg cholesterol, 565mg sodium

> **TIP:** If you'd like, double the tomato-olive mixture and toss half with 8 ounces cooked corkscrew pasta. Serve the pasta at room temperature alongside the chicken.

Lemon-Oregano Chicken with Mint Zucchini

For even cooking, it's a good idea to pound chicken breasts to a uniform thickness. See the box on page 57 for directions on how to do it.

PREP: 15 minutes   **GRILL:** 8 to 12 minutes
MAKES: 4 main-dish servings

3	medium zucchini (8 ounces each)
2	tablespoons olive oil
$\frac{1}{2}$	teaspoon salt
$\frac{1}{2}$	cup loosely packed fresh mint leaves, chopped
4	medium skinless, boneless chicken-breast halves (about 1$\frac{1}{2}$ pounds total)
3	lemons
1	tablespoon chopped fresh oregano
$\frac{1}{2}$	teaspoon coarsely ground black pepper

1. Prepare outdoor grill for direct grilling over medium heat, or lightly spray a ridged grill pan with nonstick cooking spray, then heat on medium until hot.

2. With mandoline or sharp knife, slice zucchini very thinly lengthwise. In large bowl, toss zucchini with 1 tablespoon oil, $\frac{1}{4}$ teaspoon salt, and half of mint.

3. Pound chicken breasts to uniform $\frac{1}{4}$-inch thickness. From 2 lemons, grate 1 tablespoon peel and squeeze 2 tablespoons juice. Cut remaining lemon into 4 wedges; set aside. In medium bowl, combine lemon peel and juice with oregano, pepper, and remaining 1 tablespoon oil and $\frac{1}{4}$ teaspoon salt. Add chicken to bowl and toss until evenly coated.

4. Place zucchini slices, in batches, on hot grill rack and cook until grill marks appear and zucchini is tender, 2 to 4 minutes, turning over once. Remove zucchini from grill; place on large platter and sprinkle with remaining mint.

5. Place chicken on hot grill rack or pan. Cover and cook until juices run clear when chicken is pierced with tip of knife, 6 to 8 minutes, turning over once. Transfer chicken to platter with zucchini; serve with lemon wedges.

EACH SERVING: About 280 calories, 42g protein, 8g carbohydrate, 9g total fat (2g saturated), 99mg cholesterol, 390mg sodium

Poultry Safety Strategies

Chicken and turkey are deliciously simple choices for dinner, but because of the possibility of salmonella, they need to be treated with respect. Here are some sensible tips for keeping it safe in the kitchen and on the grill:

PROMOTE GOOD HYGIENE: **Proper hand washing—20 seconds with hot, soapy water—is absolutely essential before and after handling raw poultry. Try this tactic: Wash as long as it takes to sing two rousing choruses of "Happy Birthday." You may even encourage good hygiene in your child with this tactic!**

TACKLE CROSS-CONTAMINATION: **Place the package of raw poultry in a plastic bag to separate it from other groceries. Take it straight home from the store and refrigerate it immediately (35° to 40°F). Set wrapped raw poultry on a plate on the bottom shelf of the refrigerator so juices don't drip onto other foods. Always thoroughly wash cutting boards, knives, utensils, and countertops after they come in contact with raw poultry. Never place cooked food on a plate that previously held raw poultry.**

MAKE SEASONING SAFE: **Always marinate in the refrigerator. If using a marinade as a basting or dipping sauce, set aside a portion before adding the raw food. Wash basting brushes with hot, soapy water after using them on poultry. Discard leftover marinade that comes in contact with raw poultry, or bring it to a boil for 1 minute before serving.**

REFRIGERATE OR COOK: **Thaw poultry in the refrigerator or in the microwave; never leave it at room temperature. When you thaw in the microwave, cook the poultry immediately and completely to destroy harmful bacteria. Never partially grill and finish cooking it later.**

Coffee-Spice Chicken and Fruit-Basil Salsa

A jerk-style seasoning of allspice and java gives this Caribbean chicken its caffeinated kick. Balancing the heat: a cooling summer salsa of just-picked nectarines and juicy watermelon.

PREP: 30 minutes   GRILL: 8 to 10 minutes
MAKES: 8 main-dish servings

3   cups seedless watermelon cubes, cut into ½-inch chunks (from 4-pound piece of watermelon)
1   large ripe nectarine, pitted and cut into ½-inch chunks
3   tablespoons finely chopped red onion
1   tablespoon fresh lemon juice
2   tablespoons instant coffee
1   tablespoon grated peeled fresh ginger
1   tablespoon olive oil
1¼ teaspoons ground allspice
¾   teaspoon salt
8   skinless, boneless chicken-breast halves (about 3 pounds total)
½   cup packed fresh basil leaves, coarsely chopped

1. In medium bowl, combine watermelon, nectarine, red onion, and lemon juice. Cover and refrigerate salsa while preparing chicken. Makes 4 cups.

2. Prepare outdoor grill for direct grilling over medium heat, or lightly spray a ridged grill pan with nonstick cooking spray, then heat on medium until hot.

3. In large bowl, with spoon or fingers, press coffee to pulverize. Add ginger, oil, allspice, and ½ teaspoon salt; stir to combine. Add chicken and toss to evenly coat with spice mixture (you may need to pat spice mixture onto chicken with fingers).

4. Place chicken breasts on hot grill grate or pan. Cover and cook 8 to 10 minutes or until juices run clear when thickest part of chicken is pierced with tip of knife, turning once. Transfer chicken to cutting board and let rest 5 minutes. Meanwhile, stir basil and remaining ¼ teaspoon salt into salsa. Slice chicken crosswise and serve with salsa alongside.

EACH SERVING: About 235 calories, 40g protein, 8g carbohydrate, 4g total fat (1g saturated), 99mg cholesterol, 310mg sodium

Charcoal-Grilled Turkey

Cooking a turkey on a covered charcoal grill gives it a delightful smoky flavor. Using an outdoor grill also frees up the kitchen for other holiday dinner preparations, and it cuts down considerably on cleanup.

PREP: **15 minutes**
GRILL: **2 hours 30 minutes to 3 hours**
MAKES: **16 main-dish servings**

2   cups mesquite chips
1   turkey (12 pounds), fresh or frozen (thawed)
1 to 2 (8-inch) metal skewers and kitchen string or stuffing clamp
2   tablespoons vegetable oil
2   teaspoons dried rosemary, crumbled
2   teaspoons dried thyme
2   teaspoons salt
½   teaspoon ground black pepper
rosemary sprigs for garnish

1. Soak mesquite chips in enough *water* to cover for about 1 hour.

2. To prepare coals: In bottom of covered charcoal grill, with vents open and grill uncovered, ignite 60 charcoal briquettes (not self-starting). Allow briquettes to burn until all coals are covered with a thin coating of gray ash, about 30 minutes. Push hot briquettes to two sides of grill; place sturdy disposable foil pan (about 13″ by 9″ by 2″) in between coals. Drain chips well and scatter over hot coals.

3. Meanwhile, remove giblets and neck from turkey; reserve for use in soup another day. Rinse turkey with cold running water and drain well. Fasten neck skin to back with 1 or 2 skewers. With turkey breast side up, fold wings under back of turkey so they stay in place. Depending on brand of turkey, with string, tie legs and tail together, or push drumsticks under band of skin, or use stuffing clamp. In cup, mix oil, dried rosemary, thyme, salt, and pepper; rub mixture all over turkey.

4. Place turkey, breast side up, on hot grill rack directly over foil pan (to catch drips). Cover grill and roast turkey 2 hours 15 minutes to 3 hours (11 to 13 minutes per pound for unstuffed bird), adding 8 to 9 briquettes to each side of pan every hour to maintain a grill temperature of 325°F on oven or grill thermometer. Turkey is done when thigh temperature on meat thermometer reaches 175 to 180°F and juices run clear when thickest part of thigh is pierced with tip of knife; breast temperature should reach 165 to 170°F. (Upon standing, temperature will rise 5 to 10°F.)

5. When turkey is done, place on cutting board; let stand 15 minutes to allow juices to set for easier carving. Carefully remove drip pan from grill; skim fat from drippings. Carve turkey and arrange on warm large platter; garnish with rosemary sprigs. Serve drippings along with turkey.

EACH SERVING: About 250 calories, 43g protein, 0g carbohydrate, 8g total fat (2g saturated), 112mg cholesterol, 190mg sodium

Spiced Grilled Turkey Breast

Soaking a whole turkey breast overnight in a spiced salt solution, or brine, produces exceptionally tender and flavorful meat. You can also brine a whole chicken before roasting.

PREP: 35 minutes plus brining and standing
GRILL: 25 to 30 minutes

MAKES: 12 main-dish servings

SPICED TURKEY BREAST

¼	cup sugar
¼	cup kosher salt
2	tablespoons cracked black pepper
2	tablespoons ground ginger
1	tablespoon ground cinnamon
4	cups water
1	whole boneless turkey breast (about 4 pounds), skin removed, breast cut in half
4	garlic cloves, crushed with side of chef's knife

CHIPOTLE HONEY MUSTARD GLAZE

2	tablespoons honey
2	tablespoons Dijon mustard
1	chipotle chile in adobo, minced
1	teaspoon balsamic vinegar
1	recipe Peach Salsa (page 136)

1. Prepare turkey: In 2-quart saucepan, heat sugar, salt, pepper, ginger, cinnamon, and 1 cup water to boiling over high heat. Reduce heat to low; simmer 2 minutes. Meanwhile, stir remaining water with ice cubes to chill. Remove pan from heat; stir in 3 cups ice water.

2. Place turkey breast in large zip-tight plastic bag; add brine and garlic. Seal bag, pressing out excess air. Place bag in bowl and refrigerate, turning occasionally, 24 hours.

3. Prepare outdoor grill for covered direct grilling over medium heat. With long-handled basting brush, oil grill rack.

4. Meanwhile, prepare glaze: In small bowl, stir honey, mustard, chipotle, and vinegar until blended. Set aside.

5. Remove turkey from bag and discard brine and garlic. With paper towels, pat turkey dry and brush off most of pepper. Place turkey on hot grill rack. Cover grill and cook turkey 20 minutes, turning over once. Brush turkey with glaze and cook 5 to 10 minutes longer (depending on thickness of breast), brushing and turning frequently, until temperature on instant-read meat thermometer inserted into thickest part of breast reaches 165°F. (Internal temperature will rise 5°F upon standing.) Place turkey on cutting board and let stand 10 minutes to allow juices to set for easier slicing.

6. While turkey rests, prepare Peach Salsa.

7. Serve turkey hot, or cover and refrigerate to serve cold, with the salsa on the side.

EACH SERVING TURKEY: About 170 calories, 34g protein, 4g carbohydrate, 1g total fat (0g saturated), 94mg cholesterol, 555mg sodium

Prosciutto-Wrapped Turkey Cutlets with Basil-Melon Salsa

When buying turkey cutlets for this recipe, make sure not to get the ones that are very thinly sliced for scaloppine.

PREP: 20 minutes **GRILL:** 5 to 7 minutes

MAKES: 4 main-dish servings

2	limes
1½	cups chopped, peeled cantaloupe
1½	cups chopped, peeled honeydew melon
1	small Kirby cucumber, shredded (½ cup)
1	jalapeño chile, seeded and finely chopped
¼	cup loosely packed fresh basil leaves, chopped
¼	teaspoon salt
4	turkey breast cutlets (1 pound total)
¼	teaspoon coarsely ground black pepper
4	ounces thinly sliced prosciutto

1. Grease grill rack. Prepare outdoor grill for direct grilling over medium heat, or lightly spray a ridged grill pan with nonstick cooking spray, then heat on medium until hot.

2. From 1 lime, grate 1 teaspoon peel and squeeze 2 tablespoons juice. Cut remaining lime into 4 wedges and set aside. In medium bowl, combine lime juice, cantaloupe, honeydew, cucumber, jalapeño, basil, and salt. Makes about 3 cups salsa.

3. Sprinkle turkey cutlets with lime peel and pepper. Wrap cutlets with prosciutto, pressing prosciutto firmly to turkey.

4. Place cutlets on hot grill rack or pan and cook until turkey loses its pink color throughout, 5 to 7 minutes, turning over once. Transfer turkey to plate; serve with salsa and lime wedges.

EACH SERVING TURKEY: About 185 calories, 35g protein, 0g carbohydrate, 4g total fat (1g saturated), 86mg cholesterol, 815mg sodium

EACH ¼ CUP SALSA: About 10 calories, 0g protein, 3g carbohydrate, 0g total fat, 0mg cholesterol, 50mg sodium

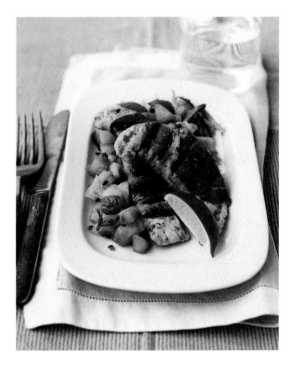

Orange-Rosemary Turkey Cutlets with Couscous and Arugula

Turkey cutlets keep this dish lean, while flavor-packed citrus and rosemary keep guests coming back for more.

PREP: 15 minutes   **GRILL: 4 to 5 minutes**
MAKES: 4 main-dish servings

3   navel oranges
1½ cups water
3   tablespoons olive oil
½   teaspoon salt
1½ cups whole-wheat couscous
1   tablespoon fresh rosemary leaves, chopped
¼   teaspoon ground black pepper
4   turkey cutlets (1 pound total)
2   tablespoons seasoned rice vinegar
1   bag (5 ounces) baby arugula

1. From oranges, grate 2 tablespoons peel and squeeze ³/₄ cup juice. In 4-quart saucepan, heat water, ¹/₂ cup orange juice, 1 tablespoon orange peel, 2 teaspoons oil, and ¹/₄ teaspoon salt to boiling over high heat. Stir in couscous; cover saucepan and remove from heat. Let stand until ready to serve.

2. Heat ridged grill pan over medium-high heat, or prepare outdoor grill for direct grilling over medium-high heat. In cup, combine remaining 1 tablespoon orange peel with rosemary, 1 teaspoon oil, remaining ¹/₄ teaspoon salt, and pepper. Pat turkey cutlets dry with paper towels, then rub both sides of each cutlet with rosemary mixture.

3. Add cutlets to hot grill pan or rack and cook until cutlets just lose their pink color throughout, 4 to 5 minutes, turning over once.

4. In small bowl, prepare orange vinaigrette: Whisk together vinegar and remaining ¹/₄ cup orange juice; slowly whisk in remaining 2 tablespoons oil until blended.

5. To serve, fluff couscous with fork. Toss arugula with ¹/₄ cup vinaigrette. Arrange arugula on 4 dinner plates; top with couscous and turkey. Drizzle with remaining vinaigrette.

EACH SERVING: About 410 calories, 33g protein, 44g carbohydrate, 12g total fat (2g saturated), 71mg cholesterol, 610mg sodium

Beef, Veal, Lamb, and Pork

Steak was made for the grill. With a flame-charred outside and tender pink inside it's irresistible. If cooking the perfect steak has eluded you, you'll find plenty of help in this chapter: tips for grilling, a chart with grill times, and advice for determining doneness, plus a mouthwatering collection of recipes for every kind of beef steak—filet mignon, sirloin, Porterhouse, flank, and skirt.

Veal isn't something you often see on the grill, but we have some great options. And if you haven't tried lamb on the grill, make sure you do—whether you choose a recipe for butterflied leg of lamb or kabobs, the flavor is superb. Pork in all its forms is extremely versatile when it comes to the grill and the grill pan, whether it be a roast, tenderloin, chops, ribs, or kabobs. A single pork tenderloin will feed a family of four nicely, cooks up in just 20 minutes, and takes to a wide range of flavors.

Filet Mignon with Horseradish Salsa, page 74

Spice-Rubbed Beef Tenderloin

Make a double batch of this rub and use it the next time you're grilling pork chops, pork tenderloin, or a leg of lamb.

PREP: 10 minutes plus standing
GRILL: 30 to 40 minutes

MAKES: 10 main-dish servings

1	tablespoon fennel seeds
2	teaspoons salt
½	teaspoon ground ginger
½	teaspoon crushed red pepper
1	beef tenderloin roast (about 2½ pounds; see Tip)

1. Prepare outdoor grill for covered direct grilling over medium heat.

2. In mortar with pestle or in zip-tight plastic bag with rolling pin, crush fennel seeds. In small bowl, combine fennel seeds, salt, ginger, and crushed red pepper.

3. Rub beef tenderloin with spice mixture. Place spice-rubbed beef in zip-tight plastic bag and refrigerate several hours or overnight before grilling.

4. Place beef on hot grill rack. Cover grill and cook beef, turning occasionally, until meat thermometer inserted in center reaches 135°F, 30 to 40 minutes. Internal temperature of meat will rise to 140°F (medium-rare) upon standing. Or cook until meat reaches desired doneness. Transfer to cutting board and let stand 10 minutes to set juices for easier slicing.

EACH SERVING: About 225 calories, 19g protein, 0g carbohydrate, 16g total fat (6g saturated), 66mg cholesterol, 510mg sodium

> **TIP:** Ask your butcher to cut this roast from a whole tenderloin for you. The center-cut roast should be 2½ pounds after trimming; the ends make deliciously tender kabobs.

GRILLING BEEF

To test for doneness, insert an instant-read meat thermometer into the center or thickest part of the meat. If it is ½ inch thick or less, insert the thermometer horizontally into the meat, halfway in. Always let steak rest approximately 10 minutes before serving or slicing, so the juices have time to redistribute throughout the meat. During the resting time, the internal temperature of the meat will rise about 5 degrees.

CUT	COOK-TO INTERNAL TEMPERATURE	APPROXIMATE COOK TIME
Steaks (porterhouse, T-bone, sirloin, rib-eye, top round):		
¾" thick	145°F	6–8 minutes
1" thick	145°F	11–14 minutes
Steaks (flank or skirt)	145°F	15–20 minutes
Tenderloin, whole	135°F	30–40 minutes

Pepper-Crusted Filet Mignon

These very tender steaks are great company fare, plus they're a snap to make ahead. Simply coat them with crushed spices as directed, then cover and refrigerate for up to one day until ready to cook.

PREP: 15 minutes plus standing
GRILL: 16 to 20 minutes
MAKES: 4 main-dish servings

1	tablespoon whole black peppercorns
1	teaspoon fennel seeds
4	beef tenderloin steaks (filet mignon), 1 inch thick (about 4 ounces each)
3	medium peppers (red, yellow, and/or orange), each stemmed, seeded, and cut in half lengthwise
1	tablespoon minced fresh parsley
1	teaspoon olive oil
¾	teaspoon salt

1. Prepare outdoor grill for covered direct grilling over medium-high heat, or lightly spray a ridged grill pan with nonstick cooking spray, then heat on medium until hot.

2. Meanwhile, in mortar with pestle or in zip-tight plastic bag with rolling pin, crush peppercorns and fennel seeds. With hands, pat spice mixture around edges of steaks. Cover and refrigerate steaks until ready to cook. If you like, steaks can be prepared up to 1 day ahead.

3. With hand, flatten each pepper half and place, skin side down, on hot grill rack or pan. Cover and cook until skins are charred and blistered, 8 to 10 minutes. Transfer peppers to bowl; cover with plate and let steam at room temperature until cool enough to handle, about 15 minutes. If using gas grill, reset temperature to medium.

4. Remove peppers from bowl. Peel skins and discard. Cut peppers lengthwise into ¼-inch-wide strips. Return peppers to same bowl and toss with parsley, oil, and ¼ teaspoon salt.

5. Sprinkle steaks with remaining ½ teaspoon salt. Place steaks on hot grill rack. Cover grill and cook, turning once, 8 to 10 minutes for medium-rare or until desired doneness. Serve steaks topped with peppers.

EACH SERVING: About 230 calories, 26g protein, 9g carbohydrate, 10g total fat (3g saturated), 71mg cholesterol, 495mg sodium

Filet Mignon with Roquefort

Tangy Roquefort cheese is such a luxuriously flavorful topping that just a tablespoon per serving is enough.

PREP: 5 minutes   **GRILL: 10 minutes**
MAKES: 4 main-dish servings

4   beef tenderloin steaks (filet mignon),
      1 inch thick (4 ounces each)
2   teaspoons olive oil
½   teaspoon salt
¼   teaspoon coarsely ground pepper
1   ounce Roquefort cheese, crumbled (¼ cup)

1. Heat ridged grill pan on medium-high heat until hot, or prepare outdoor grill for direct grilling over medium-high heat. Pat steaks dry with paper towels. Rub oil all over steaks and sprinkle with salt and pepper.

2. Place steaks in hot grill pan or on hot rack and cook 8 to 10 minutes for medium-rare, or to desired doneness, turning over once. Transfer steaks to 4 dinner plates; top with Roquefort.

EACH SERVING: About 205 calories, 25g protein, 0g carbohydrate, 11g total fat (4g saturated), 63mg cholesterol, 470mg sodium

Filet Mignon with Horseradish Salsa

Juicy steaks taste even better with our flavor-packed salsa. (For photo, see page 70.) For an extra-special company dinner, grill portobello mushrooms as you would in Portobello and Prosciutto Salad (page 57) and serve thickly sliced alongside.

PREP: 15 minutes   **GRILL: 10 to 12 minutes**
MAKES: 4 main-dish servings

1   recipe Horseradish Salsa (page 135)
1   teaspoon cracked black pepper
1   teaspoon olive oil
½   teaspoon salt
¼   teaspoon dried thyme
1   garlic clove, crushed with garlic press
4   beef tenderloin steaks (filet mignon),
      1 inch thick (about 6 ounces each)

1. Prepare Horseradish Salsa.

2. Prepare outdoor grill for direct grilling over medium heat, or lightly spray a ridged grill pan with nonstick cooking spray, then heat on medium until hot.

3. In cup, mix pepper, oil, salt, thyme, and garlic. Rub pepper mixture all over steaks.

4. Place steaks on hot grill rack or pan and grill, turning over once, 10 to 12 minutes for medium-rare or until desired doneness. Serve steaks with Horseradish Salsa.

EACH SERVING: About 330 calories, 39g protein, 9g carbohydrate, 15g total fat (4g saturated), 89mg cholesterol, 710mg sodium

The Perfect Steak

A high price alone won't guarantee great results from beef. Our tips for shopping, prepping, and cooking it right help you get the most from your splurge.

BETTER RED? Bright crimson meat has always been the standard by which a good steak is judged. But if the meat is vacuum packed, it will be purplish brown. Not to worry: Once it's exposed to oxygen, the meat will turn a satisfying red.

PAT IT DRY: To get a good sear on your steak, dry it well with paper towels. If there's any surface moisture, the meat will steam, not brown.

SLASH THE FAT? Today most meat is trimmed, leaving only ¼ inch of fat, so there's no need to make slashes in the fat to keep the steak from curling as it cooks. If your butcher does leave on a thicker layer, you can make shallow vertical slits in the fat, taking care not to cut through to the meat.

A TIME TO SEASON: Don't salt in advance—you'll draw out the juices. Preheat your grill or pan, then just before adding the steak, sprinkle it with salt and pepper.

CHECK FOR DONENESS: Here's a general formula for cooking a 1-inch-thick steak over medium-high heat. Rare: about 6 minutes per side (135°F). Medium: about 8 minutes per side (145°F). Well done: about 10 minutes per side (160°F). These times are only guidelines, however, so check your steak earlier to avoid overcooking it.

LEFTOVERS: Don't even try to reheat steak—the fat will oxidize, giving the meat an off flavor (think steam table). Our recommendation: Let the meat sit out of the fridge for 10 to 15 minutes, then serve it with horseradish, grainy mustard, or, if you have leftover sauce, heat it to boiling and pour it over.

Chili-Glazed Porterhouse Steak with Grilled Salad

This is steak-house fare—a big porterhouse with grilled greens on the side.

PREP: 15 minutes   GRILL: 20 to 30 minutes
MAKES: 5 main-dish servings

CHILI-GLAZED PORTERHOUSE STEAK

¼   cup chili sauce

¼   cup balsamic vinegar

¾   teaspoon salt

1   garlic clove, crushed with garlic press

1   beef loin porterhouse or T-bone steak, 2 inches thick (about 2¼ pounds)

GRILLED SALAD

1   large head radicchio, cut into 6 wedges

3   medium heads Belgian endive, each cut lengthwise in half

3   tablespoons olive oil

1   tablespoon chopped fresh rosemary leaves, or 1 teaspoon dried rosemary, crushed

½   teaspoon salt

1. Prepare outdoor grill for direct grilling over medium heat.

2. Prepare the steak: In a pie plate or deep dish, mix chili sauce, vinegar, salt, and garlic. Trim all fat from steak; add steak to chili-sauce mixture and turn to coat on both sides.

3. Place steak on hot grill rack and brush with half the chili-sauce mixture remaining in plate. Cook steak 20 to 30 minutes for medium-rare or until of desired doneness, turning steak occasionally and brushing with chili-sauce mixture remaining in plate halfway through grilling.

4. Meanwhile, prepare the salad: In small bowl, mix oil, rosemary, and salt. Place radicchio and endive on grill over medium heat with the steak; brush with olive-oil mixture. Cook, turning them occasionally, until vegetables are tender-crisp, 5 to 10 minutes.

5. Transfer steak to cutting board; let stand 10 minutes to allow juices to set for easier slicing. Slice steak and serve with the grilled salad.

EACH SERVING: About 205 calories, 22g protein, 5g carbohydrate, 10g total fat (4 saturated fat), 57mg cholesterol, 590mg sodium

Red-Wine and Rosemary Porterhouse

This robust marinade can season a thick, juicy steak in fifteen minutes. Give it up to one hour for more intense flavor. It's also good on lamb, pork, or poultry.

PREP: 10 minutes plus marinating
GRILL: 15 to 20 minutes

MAKES: 4 main-dish servings

½	cup dry red wine (see Tip)
1	tablespoon Worcestershire sauce
1	tablespoon tomato paste
1	tablespoon Dijon mustard
1	tablespoon balsamic vinegar
1	tablespoon chopped fresh rosemary
1	large garlic clove, crushed with garlic press
1	beef loin porterhouse or T-bone steak, 1½ inches thick (about 1½ pounds)
1	lemon, cut into wedges

1. In small bowl, stir together wine, Worcestershire, tomato paste, mustard, vinegar, rosemary, and garlic.

2. Place steak in large zip-tight plastic bag. Pour wine marinade over steak, turning to coat. Seal bag, pressing out excess air. Let stand 15 minutes at room temperature or refrigerate up to 1 hour, turning once.

3. Prepare outdoor grill for direct grilling over medium heat.

4. Remove steak from bag; discard marinade. Place steak on hot grill rack and grill, turning once, 15 to 20 minutes for medium-rare, or to desired doneness.

5. Transfer steak to cutting board; let stand 10 minutes to allow juices to set for easier slicing. Thinly slice steak and serve with lemon wedges.

EACH SERVING: About 395 calories, 32g protein, 1g carbohydrate, 28g total fat (11g saturated), 104mg cholesterol, 125mg sodium

> **TIP:** For a dry red wine that would work well in this recipe, try a Shiraz, Merlot, Chianti, or Cabernet.

PORTERHOUSE VERSUS T-BONE

Both steaks are cut from the beef short loin and have a T-shaped bone. But the defining characteristic is the size of the tenderloin (the smaller portion of meat on one side of the T). The T-bone's tenderloin starts at ½ inch in diameter. The more expensive porterhouse—so named because in the early 1800s, travelers dined on steak and ale at coach stops, or porter houses—contains a tenderloin that's at least 1¼ inches in diameter. Either steak works very well for our Red-Wine and Rosemary Porterhouse (above) and Chili-Glazed Porterhouse Steak with Grilled Salad (opposite).

Lemon-Soy-Marinated Sirloin Steak

Want to use a less tender cut? Marinate meat four hours or overnight to tenderize it.

PREP: 15 minutes plus marinating
GRILL: 12 to 15 minutes

MAKES: 6 main-dish servings

2	lemons
2	tablespoons soy sauce
1	tablespoon olive oil
1	clove garlic, crushed with garlic press
¼	teaspoon ground black pepper
¼	teaspoon ground red pepper (cayenne)
1	boneless beef top sirloin steak, 1¼ inches thick (about 1½ pounds)
2	tablespoons water

1. Remove 3 strips lemon peel (3″ by 1″ each) and squeeze ⅓ cup juice. In bowl, mix lemon peel and juice, soy sauce, oil, garlic, black pepper, and red pepper.

2. Pour marinade into large zip-tight plastic bag; add steak, turning to coat. Seal bag, pressing out excess air; refrigerate 30 minutes.

3. Prepare outdoor grill for direct grilling over medium heat. Remove steak from bag. Pour marinade into 1-quart saucepan, add water, and reserve.

4. Place steak on hot grill rack and cook 12 to 15 minutes for medium-rare or until desired doneness, turning once. Transfer steak to cutting board; let stand 10 minutes to allow juices to set for easier slicing.

5. Meanwhile, heat reserved marinade to boiling over high heat; boil 1 minute. To serve, thinly slice steak and serve with cooked marinade.

EACH SERVING: About 265 calories, 24g protein, 2g carbohydrate, 18g total fat (7g saturated), 77mg cholesterol, 395mg sodium

---

IS THAT STEAK DONE YET?

You've got three options when it comes to determining the doneness of a steak.

1. Using an instant-read meat thermometer, check the steak's internal temperature (see The Perfect Steak, page 75).

2. Cut a small slit in the meat near the bone or center of a boneless steak. Rare steak will be bright red in the center and pinkish toward the surface; medium-rare, very pink in the center and slightly brown toward the surface; medium, light pink in the center with a brown outer portion; and well done, brown throughout. (Unlike hamburgers, steak can safely be eaten rare or medium-rare.)

3. To test doneness without cutting, try the chef's method: Compare the feel of the meat in the top center to the skin between the thumb and index finger when your hand is relaxed (hanging loosely), lightly fisted, and tightly clenched. A rare steak feels soft and spongy when pressed, similar to a relaxed hand. A medium-rare steak is springy to the touch, as on a loosely clenched hand. Medium steak feels firm, with minimal give, like a tight fist.

Coriander Steak
with Warm Corn Salad

A simple Mexican-inspired corn salad tops luscious peppery steak.

PREP: 15 minutes   GRILL: about 8 minutes
MAKES: 4 main-dish servings

2   teaspoons olive oil

1   tablespoon coriander seeds, crushed

1   teaspoon cracked black peppercorns

3/4 teaspoon salt

2   boneless beef top sirloin steaks, 3/4 inch thick (about 10 ounces each)

1   small red pepper, stems and seeds removed, cut into 1/4-inch dice

1/2 small red onion, finely chopped

2   cups fresh corn kernels (from 4 ears)

1   tablespoon chopped fresh cilantro

1   tablespoon fresh lime juice

1/2 teaspoon ground cumin

1. Heat 10-inch ridged grill pan over medium-high heat until very hot. Brush pan with 1 teaspoon oil. On waxed paper, mix coriander, black pepper, and ¹/₂ teaspoon salt; use to coat both sides of steaks.

2. Place steaks in grill pan; cook about 8 minutes for medium-rare or until desired doneness, turning over once.

3. Meanwhile, in 2-quart saucepan, heat remaining 1 teaspoon oil over medium-high heat. Add red pepper and onion; cook until soft, about 5 minutes, stirring a few times. Add corn; heat through. Stir in cilantro, lime juice, cumin, and remaining ¹/₄ teaspoon salt. Makes about 2¹/₂ cups salad.

4. Transfer steak to cutting board; let stand 10 minutes to allow juices to set for easier slicing. Thinly slice steak and serve with corn salad.

EACH SERVING: About 430 calories, 31g protein, 25g carbohydrate, 25g total fat (9g saturated), 84mg cholesterol, 705mg sodium

> **TIP:** If you don't have a mortar and pestle to crush spices, place them in a zip-tight plastic bag. Seal the bag, then pound several times with a meat mallet, rolling pin, or heavy skillet.

Orange-Glazed Top Round Steak

We marinate the beef in a soy and garlic mixture, then brush it with orange marmalade on the grill. Serve with Orange-Chipotle Salsa (page 135) on the side.

PREP: 5 minutes plus marinating
GRILL: 20 to 25 minutes
MAKES: 6 main-dish servings

¼ cup soy sauce
2 cloves garlic, crushed with garlic press
1 teaspoon coarsely ground black pepper
1 beef top round steak, 1¼ inches thick (about 2 pounds), well trimmed
⅓ cup orange marmalade

1. In a 13" by 9" glass baking dish, mix soy sauce, garlic, and pepper. Add steak to soy sauce mixture, turning to coat. Cover and refrigerate 30 minutes, turning once.

2. Prepare outdoor grill for direct grilling over medium heat.

3. Place steak on hot grill rack; spoon remaining marinade over steak. Cook steak 20 to 25 minutes for medium-rare or until of desired doneness, brushing with orange marmalade during last 10 minutes of cooking, turning occasionally.

EACH SERVING: About 400 calories, 36g protein, 13g carbohydrate, 7g total fat (3g saturated), 95mg cholesterol, 415mg sodium

Garlic and Rosemary Flank Steak with Grilled Vegetable "Lasagna"

Add a loaf of crusty bread to round out this flavorful menu.

PREP: 30 minutes   **GRILL:** about 35 minutes
MAKES: 4 main-dish servings

1 medium red pepper
2 tablespoons soy sauce
1 tablespoon finely chopped fresh rosemary leaves
1 garlic clove, minced
5 tablespoons balsamic vinegar
4 tablespoons extra-virgin olive oil
1 beef flank steak (about 1¼ pounds), well trimmed
2 small zucchini (about 6 ounces each)
1 small yellow summer squash (about 6 ounces)
1 large portobello mushroom (about 6 ounces), stem discarded
¾ teaspoon salt
¼ teaspoon plus ⅛ teaspoon ground black pepper
2 tablespoons finely chopped fresh basil
1 tablespoon finely chopped fresh oregano
2 ounces feta cheese, crumbled (about ½ cup)
fresh rosemary sprigs for garnish

1. Heat large ridged grill pan over medium-high heat until very hot. Cut pepper lengthwise in half; discard membrane and seeds. With hand, flatten each pepper half. Place pepper halves, skin side down, in grill pan and cook until skin is charred and blistered, 3 to 4 minutes. Wrap pepper with foil; allow to steam at room temperature until cool enough to handle, about 10 minutes.

2. Meanwhile, in large zip-tight plastic bag, mix soy sauce, rosemary, garlic, 3 tablespoons vinegar, and 1 tablespoon oil. Add steak to marinade, turning to coat both sides. Seal bag, pressing out excess air. Place bag on plate and refrigerate until ready to cook.

3. Cut each zucchini and yellow squash lengthwise into 4 slices. Cut mushroom into ¹/₂-inch-thick slices. In large bowl, toss vegetables with 1 tablespoon oil, ¹/₂ teaspoon salt, and ¹/₄ teaspoon black pepper; set aside.

4. Remove red pepper from foil. Peel off skin and discard. Cut pepper into ¹/₄-inch dice. In small bowl, mix red pepper with basil, oregano, remaining 2 tablespoons vinegar, 2 tablespoons oil, ¹/₄ teaspoon salt, and ¹/₈ teaspoon black pepper. Set relish aside. Makes about 1 cup.

5. Heat same grill pan over medium-high heat until hot. Add zucchini, yellow squash, and mushroom, in batches, and cook until lightly browned on both sides and tender, about 6 minutes, turning over once. Remove vegetables to plate as they are done.

6. Remove steak from marinade; discard marinade. Pat steak dry with paper towels. In same hot grill pan over medium-high heat, cook steak 12 to 15 minutes for medium-rare or until desired doneness, turning steak over once. Transfer steak to cutting board; let rest 10 minutes to allow juices to set for easier slicing.

7. While steak is resting, assemble "lasagna": On each of 4 dinner plates, stack yellow squash, zucchini, and mushroom alternately with red-pepper relish and feta, ending with feta.

8. To serve, thinly slice steak diagonally against the grain. Arrange steak slices on plates with "lasagna." Garnish with rosemary sprigs.

EACH SERVING: About 430 calories, 33g protein, 11g carbohydrate, 28g total fat (9g saturated), 85mg cholesterol, 810mg sodium

> **TIP:** In warm weather, this recipe works well on an outdoor grill. Prepare it for direct grilling over medium-high heat. Grill as described in recipe.

Mexican Skirt Steak

Here is a flavor-packed change of pace for dinner: Garlic- and chili-rubbed beef is wrapped in warm flour tortillas with crisp lettuce and a spoonful of creamy cilantro-spiked yogurt. If skirt steak (also called top round steak) is difficult to find, flank steak is a good alternative.

PREP: 15 minutes plus standing
GRILL: 10 to 15 minutes
MAKES: 5 main-dish servings

1	lime
½	cup plain low-fat yogurt
⅓	cup chopped fresh cilantro leaves
¼	cup light mayonnaise
⅛	teaspoon plus ¾ teaspoon salt
3	tablespoons chili powder
1	teaspoon ground coriander
1	teaspoon ground cumin
1	beef skirt steak (about 1¼ pounds), well-trimmed
1	large garlic clove, cut lengthwise in half
10	(6- to 7-inch) flour tortillas
3	cups shredded romaine lettuce

1. Prepare outdoor grill for direct grilling over medium heat, or lightly spray a ridged grill pan with nonstick cooking spray, then heat on medium until hot.

2. Grate ¼ teaspoon peel and squeeze 1 teaspoon juice from lime. In small bowl, mix lime peel and juice, yogurt, cilantro, mayonnaise, and ⅛ teaspoon salt until blended. Cover and refrigerate until serving time.

3. In cup, mix chili powder, coriander, cumin, and remaining ¾ teaspoon salt. Rub steak on both sides with cut sides of garlic clove. Then rub with chili powder mixture.

4. Place steak on hot grill rack or pan and grill 5 minutes. Turn steak over and grill 5 to 10 minutes longer, for medium or until desired doneness. Transfer steak to cutting board; let stand 5 minutes to allow juices to set for easier slicing.

5. Meanwhile, wrap tortillas in foil and heat at edge of grill over low heat until heated through.

6. To serve, thinly slice steak crosswise on the diagonal. Placed sliced steak in warm tortillas; top with cilantro-yogurt sauce and lettuce.

EACH SERVING: About 450 calories, 36g protein, 40g carbohydrate, 16g total fat (5g saturated), 52 mg cholesterol, 885 mg sodium

Red Wine–Marinated London Broil

This herbed marinade not only adds flavor— it tenderizes the meat. Fresh rosemary will taste sensational, but if you can't find it, use 2 teaspoons dried rosemary, crumbled.

PREP: **10 minutes plus marinating**
GRILL: **12 to 15 minutes**
MAKES: **8 main-dish servings**

¼   cup dry red wine
2   tablespoons soy sauce
2   tablespoons balsamic vinegar
2   tablespoons chopped fresh rosemary leaves
1   tablespoon tomato paste
1   tablespoon Dijon mustard
¼   teaspoon crushed red pepper
4   large garlic cloves, crushed with garlic press
1   beef top round steak, 1 inch thick (about 2 pounds), well trimmed

1. In small bowl, with wire whisk, mix together wine, soy sauce, vinegar, rosemary, tomato paste, mustard, crushed red pepper, and garlic. Pour marinade into large zip-tight plastic bag. Add steak to marinade, turning to coat. Seal bag, pressing out excess air. Place bag on plate; refrigerate 4 to 6 hours, turning several times.

2. Prepare outdoor grill for covered direct grilling over medium heat, or lightly spray a ridged grill pan with nonstick cooking spray, then heat on medium until hot.

3. Remove steak from bag; discard marinade. Place steak on hot grill rack or pan. Cover and cook steak, turning once, 12 to 15 minutes for medium-rare or until desired doneness. Transfer steak to cutting board; let stand 10 minutes to allow juices to set for easier slicing.

4. To serve, thinly slice steak on the diagonal across the grain. Arrange on platter.

EACH SERVING: About 185 calories, 26g protein, 1g carbohydrate, 8g total fat (3g saturated), 72mg cholesterol, 115mg sodium

---

WHAT IS LONDON BROIL?

London broil was originally a recipe for a beef flank steak, which was marinated, broiled or grilled, and carved across the grain into thin slices. Despite its name, the recipe is said to be American in origin. Today the term applies not only to flank steak but also to other boneless cuts of beef such as top sirloin, top round, and chuck shoulder steaks. These are also meant to be prepared in the same manner and served thinly sliced across the grain.

Deviled Beef Short Ribs

When buying short ribs, choose the beefiest ones you can find and trim away any excess fat.

PREP: **10 minutes**   GRILL: **about 30 minutes**
MAKES: **6 main-dish servings**

⅓ cup spicy brown mustard
¼ cup prepared white horseradish
3 tablespoons Worcestershire sauce
4 pounds beef chuck short ribs, cut into serving-size pieces
unseasoned meat tenderizer
3 ripe medium tomatoes (6 to 8 ounces each), sliced (optional)

1. Prepare outdoor grill for direct grilling over medium heat, or lightly spray a ridged grill pan with nonstick cooking spray, then heat on medium until hot.

2. In small bowl, mix mustard, horseradish, and Worcestershire.

3. Sprinkle beef short ribs with meat tenderizer as label directs.

4. Place short ribs on hot grill rack. Cook about 30 minutes for medium-rare or until of desired doneness, turning ribs often and brushing with mustard mixture frequently during last 10 minutes of cooking. Serve with sliced tomatoes if you like.

EACH SERVING: About 315 calories, 31g protein, 6g carbohydrate, 18g total fat (8g saturated), 88mg cholesterol, 700mg sodium

Korean-Style Short Ribs

Marinating overnight makes these meaty ribs irresistible. Serve with a spicy cabbage slaw or a cool rice salad. If you like, sprinkle them with sesame seeds and thinly sliced green onion just before serving.

PREP: **15 minutes plus marinating overnight**
GRILL: **20 to 25 minutes**
MAKES: **6 main-dish servings**

4 pounds beef chuck short ribs, cut into 2-inch pieces
½ cup reduced-sodium soy sauce
4 teaspoons minced, peeled fresh ginger
2 teaspoons Asian sesame oil
3 large garlic cloves, minced

1. With sharp knife, cut ¼-inch-deep slashes in meaty side of short ribs at ½-inch intervals.

2. In large zip-tight plastic bag, combine soy sauce, ginger, sesame oil, and garlic. Add short ribs, turning to coat. Seal bag, pressing out as much air as possible. Place bag on plate and refrigerate overnight, turning once.

3. Prepare outdoor grill for direct grilling over medium heat.

4. Lift ribs from bag and place on hot grill rack; brush with remaining marinade in bag. Grill, turning occasionally, 20 to 25 minutes for medium-rare or until desired doneness.

EACH SERVING: About 745 calories, 34g protein, 3g carbohydrate, 65g total fat (27g saturated), 142 mg cholesterol, 880mg sodium

Brisket with Chunky BBQ Sauce

This is a great do-ahead main dish for a summer picnic. You can slow-cook the brisket on the stovetop up to several days ahead. Then, 20 minutes before serving, brush it with the sauce and grill until heated through.

PREP: 15 minutes
COOK: 3 hours   GRILL: 20 minutes
MAKES: 12 main-dish servings

1   beef brisket (4½ pounds), well trimmed
1   medium onion, cut into quarters
1   large carrot, peeled and cut
     into 1½-inch pieces
1   bay leaf
1   teaspoon whole black peppercorns
¼   teaspoon whole allspice
Chunky BBQ Sauce (page 134)

1. In 8-quart Dutch oven, place brisket, onion, carrot, bay leaf, peppercorns, and allspice. Add enough water to cover and heat to boiling over high heat. Reduce heat; cover and simmer until meat is tender, about 3 hours.

2. Meanwhile, prepare Chunky BBQ Sauce.

3. When brisket is done, transfer to large platter. If desired, cover and refrigerate until ready to serve.

4. Prepare outdoor grill for covered direct grilling over medium heat. Place brisket on hot grill rack over medium heat, cover, and cook 10 minutes. Turn brisket and cook 5 minutes longer. Spoon 1 cup barbecue sauce on top of brisket and cook until brisket is heated through, about 5 minutes longer. (Do not turn brisket after topping with sauce.) Transfer to cutting board.

6. To serve, reheat remaining sauce in small saucepan on grill. Slice brisket thinly across the grain and serve with sauce.

EACH SERVING: About 241 calories, 26g protein, 6g carbohydrate, 11g total fat (4g saturated), 81mg cholesterol, 174mg sodium

EACH ¼ CUP SAUCE: About 61 calories, 1g protein, 13g carbohydrate, 1g total fat (0g saturated), 0mg cholesterol, 328mg sodium

---

THE SKINNY ON BEEF RIBS

You know, it's not all about pork when you're talking ribs. Here are some tasty beef alternatives when you're looking for something a little different:

■ **Beef back ribs** are the large bones left when a standing rib roast is cut to make a boneless rib-eye roast. The ribs are trimmed and divided into single-rib portions.

■ **Short ribs,** cut from the shoulder, are rectangular. They contain a cross section of rib bones with alternating layers of lean meat and fat.

■ **Flanken-style ribs** are similar to short ribs (they're from the same area of the cow) but are cut across rather than between the ribs.

Stuffed Veal Chops

Thick, juicy veal chops, stuffed with a mixture of creamy cheese, roasted peppers, and basil, sit atop a bed of spicy greens. The combination of warm chop and cool greens is a real winner. Use a small paring knife to cut the pocket so that it is deep but not wide.

PREP: 15 minutes   **GRILL:** 10 to 12 minutes
MAKES: 4 main-dish servings

¼ cup store-bought roasted red peppers, drained and chopped

3 tablespoons chopped fresh basil

4 veal rib chops, 1 inch thick (about 10 ounces each)

2 ounces Fontina cheese, sliced

½ plus ⅛ teaspoon salt

½ plus ⅛ teaspoon coarsely ground black pepper

1 tablespoon olive oil

1 tablespoon balsamic vinegar

½ teaspoon Dijon mustard

4 ounces arugula, watercress, or baby spinach, trimmed

1. Prepare outdoor grill for direct grilling over medium-high heat, or lightly spray a ridged grill pan with nonstick cooking spray, then heat on medium until hot.

2. In small bowl, mix roasted red peppers and 2 tablespoons basil. Set aside.

3. Holding knife parallel to surface, cut a horizontal pocket in each chop. Tuck cheese slices into veal pockets; spread red-pepper mixture over cheese. Sprinkle veal chops with ½ teaspoon salt and ½ teaspoon pepper.

4. Place chops on hot grill rack or pan and grill, turning chops once, until they are lightly browned on both sides and just lose their pink color throughout, 10 to 12 minutes.

5. Meanwhile, in medium bowl, with wire whisk, mix oil, vinegar, mustard, and remaining 1 tablespoon basil, ⅛ teaspoon salt, and ⅛ teaspoon pepper; add arugula, tossing to coat.

6. To serve, spoon salad onto platter; arrange chops on top.

EACH SERVING: About 440 calories, 40g protein, 2g carbohydrate, 29g total fat (11g saturated), 181mg cholesterol, 655mg sodium

Spicy Garlic Lamb with Minted Cucumber Raita

Leg of lamb isn't only for the oven; it's divine cooked on the grill. The raita—cucumbers in minted yogurt—balances the spicy meat.

PREP: 30 minutes plus chilling
GRILL: 15 to 25 minutes

MAKES: 8 main-dish servings

MINTED CUCUMBER RAITA

6   Kirby cucumbers (about 1½ pounds)
1   teaspoon salt
2   cups (16 ounces) plain low-fat yogurt
½   cup loosely packed fresh mint leaves, chopped
1½ teaspoons sugar

SPICY GARLIC LAMB

1   tablespoon fennel seeds
1   tablespoon mustard seeds
1   tablespoon cumin seeds
2   teaspoons salt
1   teaspoon whole black peppercorns
1   teaspoon dried thyme
3   whole cloves
3   garlic cloves, crushed with garlic press
2   tablespoons fresh lemon juice
1   butterflied boneless leg of lamb (3½ pounds) trimmed

mint sprigs for garnish

1. Prepare raita: With vegetable peeler, remove several strips of peel from each cucumber. Cut each cucumber lengthwise in half; scoop out seeds; cut each piece lengthwise in half again, then crosswise into ½-inch-thick pieces. In medium bowl, toss cucumbers with ¼ teaspoon salt; let stand 10 minutes. Press cucumbers to remove as much liquid as possible. Stir in yogurt, mint, sugar, and remaining ¾ teaspoon salt. Cover and refrigerate until ready to serve or up to 6 hours. Makes about 4 cups.

2. Prepare outdoor grill for direct grilling over medium-low heat.

3. Prepare lamb: In spice grinder or coffee grinder, blend fennel, mustard, cumin, salt, peppercorns, thyme, and cloves until finely ground.

4. In small bowl, mix garlic and lemon juice with ground spices until blended. Rub spice mixture over both sides of lamb.

5. Place lamb on hot grill rack; cover and cook 15 to 25 minutes for medium-rare or until desired doneness, turning lamb once. Thickness of butterflied lamb will vary throughout; cut off sections of lamb as they are cooked and place on cutting board. Let stand 10 minutes to allow juices to set for easier slicing.

6. To serve, thinly slice lamb and arrange on platter; garnish with mint sprigs. Serve with Minted Cucumber Raita.

EACH SERVING LAMB: About 275 calories, 39g protein, 2g carbohydrate, 11g total fat (4g saturated), 121mg cholesterol, 675mg sodium

EACH ½ CUP RAITA: About 60 calories, 4g protein, 10g carbohydrate, 2g total fat (0g saturated), 4mg cholesterol, 260mg sodium

Butterflied Leg of Lamb with Almond-Mint Pesto

We top this juicy, chargrilled leg of lamb with our fresh mint-and-almond pesto—a flavor match made in heaven. The thickness of a butterflied leg of lamb will vary; check thinner pieces early for doneness, cut off those sections as they are cooked, and place them on a cutting board. Cover with foil to keep warm.

PREP: **10 minutes plus marinating**
GRILL: **15 to 25 minutes**
MAKES: **12 main-dish servings**

4 1/2 cups loosely packed fresh mint leaves

2 garlic cloves, crushed with garlic press

1/2 cup water

1/3 cup olive oil

1 teaspoon salt

1 teaspoon coarsely ground black pepper

1 butterflied boneless leg of lamb (4 pounds), trimmed

3/4 cup whole blanched almonds

1. In food processor with knife blade attached, pulse mint, garlic, water, oil, salt, and pepper until well blended.

2. Place lamb in 13″ by 9″ glass baking dish. Remove 1/4 cup mint mixture from food processor; spread on lamb to coat both sides. Cover and refrigerate at least 1 hour or up to 6 hours.

3. Meanwhile, add almonds to mint mixture remaining in food processor and pulse until almonds are finely chopped. Spoon pesto into serving bowl; cover and refrigerate until ready to serve.

4. Remove lamb from refrigerator about 15 minutes before cooking. Prepare outdoor grill for covered direct grilling over medium heat.

5. Place lamb on hot grill rack; cover and cook 15 to 25 minutes (depending on thickness) for medium-rare, turning over once halfway through cooking and removing pieces to cutting board as they are done. When remaining lamb is done, transfer to same cutting board and let stand 10 minutes to allow juices to set for easier slicing. Serve lamb with almond-mint pesto.

EACH SERVING: About 380 calories, 32g protein, 5g carbohydrate, 26g total fat (8g saturated), 99mg cholesterol, 270mg sodium

Aromatic Leg of Lamb

Once your butcher has boned a leg of lamb for you, ask for the lamb bone. Use it to cook up some flavorful lamb broth for an especially tasty stew or hearty soup.

PREP: 20 minutes **GRILL:** 15 to 25 minutes
MAKES: 8 main-dish servings

1   butterflied boneless leg of lamb (3 pounds), trimmed
3   garlic cloves, each cut in half and crushed with side of chef's knife
1   tablespoon olive oil
2   teaspoons fennel seeds, crushed
2   teaspoons cumin seeds, crushed
2   teaspoons coriander seeds, crushed
1½   teaspoons salt
1   lemon, cut into wedges

1. Prepare outdoor grill for covered direct grilling over medium heat. Rub both sides of lamb with cut sides of garlic cloves; discard garlic.

2. In small bowl, combine oil, fennel seeds, cumin seeds, coriander seeds, and salt. Use to rub on lamb.

3. Place lamb on hot grill rack, cover and cook, turning lamb occasionally, 15 to 25 minutes for medium-rare or until desired doneness. Thickness of butterflied lamb will vary throughout; cut off sections of lamb as they are done and place on cutting board. Let stand 10 minutes to allow juices to set for easier slicing. Thinly slice the lamb and serve with lemon wedges.

EACH SERVING: About 265 calories, 36g protein, 1g carbohydrate, 12g total fat (4g saturated), 114mg cholesterol, 525mg sodium

Grilled Lamb Chops with Spice Rub

Grilling chops that have been seasoned with a rub is the easiest way to guarantee lots of flavor.

PREP: 5 minutes **GRILL:** about 10 minutes
MAKES: 4 main-dish servings

1   recipe choice of dry spice rub (pages 132-133)
4   lamb shoulder chops, ¾ inch thick (each 8 ounces)

1. Prepare outdoor grill for direct grilling over medium heat.

2. In small bowl, combine rub ingredients; use to rub on lamb chops.

3. Place chops on hot grill rack and cook about 5 minutes per side for medium-rare or until desired doneness.

EACH SERVING: About 454 calories, 57g protein, 2g carbohydrate, 22g total fat (8g saturated), 196mg cholesterol, 470mg sodium

Hoisin-Honey-Glazed Pork Tenderloin with Grilled Pineapple

When choosing a pineapple, pick one that is slightly soft with a deep, sweet fragrance. Pineapples are harvested ripe and will not get any sweeter with time.

PREP: 10 minutes   GRILL: 18 to 20 minutes
MAKES: 4 main-dish servings

¼   cup hoisin sauce
1   tablespoon honey
1   tablespoon grated, peeled fresh ginger
1   teaspoon Asian sesame oil
1   pork tenderloin (1¼ pounds), trimmed
½   medium pineapple
2   tablespoons brown sugar

1. Prepare outdoor grill for covered direct grilling over medium heat. In small bowl, combine hoisin sauce, honey, ginger, and sesame oil.

2. Place pork on hot grill rack. Cover grill and cook pork 18 to 20 minutes, turning occasionally, until browned outside and still slightly pink in center; an instant-read meat thermometer inserted in thickest part of tenderloin should read 150°F.

3. Meanwhile, with serrated knife, cut pineapple half into 4 wedges. Rub cut sides of pineapple with brown sugar.

4. Grill pineapple on rack with pork until browned on both sides, about 5 minutes, turning over once. While pineapple is grilling, brush pork with hoisin-honey glaze and turn frequently.

5. Transfer pork to cutting board; let stand 5 minutes to allow juices to set for easier slicing. Transfer pineapple to platter. Thinly slice pork and serve with pineapple wedges.

EACH SERVING: About 275 calories, 31g protein, 23g carbohydrate, 6g total fat (2g saturated), 92mg cholesterol, 245mg sodium

GRILLING PORK

Our top tip for succulent pork is not to overcook it. Use an instant-read meat thermometer to check the internal temperature.

CUT	COOK-TO INTERNAL TEMPERATURE	APPROXIMATE COOK TIME
Chops (rib or loin, 1" thick)	150°F	10-12 minutes
Tenderloin, whole (1 to 1¼ pounds)	150°F	13-23 minutes
Tenderloin steaks, ¼" thick	150°F	5-6 minutes

Pork Tenderloins with Oregano

A lemon-herb marinade gives this lean cut of pork a zippy flavor. Twenty minutes is all it needs; the lemon juice will start to break down the meat fibers if it marinates much longer.

PREP: **10 minutes plus marinating**
GRILL: **15 to 20 minutes**
MAKES: **6 main-dish servings**

¼   cup fresh lemon juice

2   tablespoons chopped fresh oregano
     or 1 teaspoon dried oregano

2   tablespoons chopped fresh parsley

2   pork tenderloins (about 12 ounces each),
     trimmed

1   tablespoon olive oil

½   teaspoon salt

¼   teaspoon coarsely ground black pepper

1. In large zip-tight plastic bag, combine lemon juice and 1 tablespoon each oregano and parsley. Add tenderloins, turning to coat. Seal bag, pressing out excess air. Place bag on plate; refrigerate 20 minutes to marinate, turning once.

2. Prepare outdoor grill for direct grilling over medium heat, or lightly spray a ridged grill pan with nonstick cooking spray, then heat on medium until hot.

3. Remove tenderloins from bag; discard marinade. In cup, mix oil, salt, pepper, and remaining 1 tablespoon each oregano and parsley; rub mixture on tenderloins.

4. Place tenderloins on hot grill rack or pan and grill 20 minutes, turning occasionally, until browned outside and still slightly pink in center; an instant-read meat thermometer inserted in thickest part of tenderloin should register 150°F.

5. When tenderloins are done, transfer to warm large platter and let stand 5 minutes to allow juices to set for easier slicing. Thinly slice tenderloins to serve.

EACH SERVING: About 175 calories, 23g protein, 1g carbohydrate, 8g total fat (3g saturated), 71mg cholesterol, 240mg sodium

> **TIP:** To prevent bacterial contamination from raw meat, always follow the "two-platter" rule: Use one platter for transporting meat, poultry, or fish to the grill, then use a second, clean one for the cooked food.

Bacon-Wrapped Maple-Glazed Pork Tenderloins

Use leftovers for a sandwich treat of thinly sliced pork topped with sharp Cheddar cheese and apple slices.

PREP: 10 minutes, plus refrigerating
GRILL: 20 to 25 minutes

MAKES: 6 main-dish servings

2	pork tenderloins (12 ounces each), trimmed
8	wooden toothpicks
½	teaspoon salt
¼	teaspoon ground black pepper
6	slices bacon
½	cup maple or maple-flavored syrup

1. Prepare outdoor grill for direct grilling over medium heat. Soak toothpicks in water for 30 minutes.

2. Sprinkle tenderloins with salt and pepper. Place pork in bowl; cover and refrigerate 30 minutes.

3. Wrap 3 bacon slices around each tenderloin and secure with toothpicks. Place tenderloins on hot grill rack over medium heat and cook, brushing frequently with syrup and turning occasionally, until browned on the outside and still slightly pink in the center, 20 to 25 minutes; an instant-read meat thermometer inserted in thickest part of tenderloin should register 150°F. Transfer to cutting board and let stand 5 minutes to allow juices to set for easier slicing.

EACH SERVING: About 265 calories, 28g protein, 18g carbohydrate, 9g total fat (3g saturated), 86mg cholesterol, 352mg sodium

Spiced Pork Tenderloin Cutlets with Mango-Kiwi Salsa

A simple blend of warm spices lends exotic flavor to lean and tender pork "cutlets."

PREP: 20 minutes   GRILL: 6 to 7 minutes

MAKES: 8 main-dish servings

	Mango-Kiwi Salsa (page 137)
2	pork tenderloins (about 1 pound each), trimmed
3	tablespoons all-purpose flour
1	teaspoon salt
1	teaspoon ground cumin
1	teaspoon ground coriander
½	teaspoon ground cinnamon
½	teaspoon ground ginger

1. Prepare Mango-Kiwi Salsa; cover and refrigerate. Prepare outdoor grill for direct grilling over medium heat.

2. Cut each pork tenderloin lengthwise almost in half, being careful not to cut all the way through. Open and spread flat. Place each tenderloin between two sheets of plastic wrap; with meat mallet or rolling pin, pound to ¼-inch thickness. Cut each tenderloin into 4 pieces. On waxed paper, mix flour, salt, cumin, coriander, cinnamon, and ginger; evenly coat pork cutlets.

3. Place pork on hot grill rack over medium heat and grill until lightly browned on both sides and pork just loses its pink color throughout, 6 to 7 minutes, turning over once. Serve with Mango-Kiwi Salsa.

EACH SERVING: About 215 calories, 23g protein, 15g carbohydrate, 6g total fat (2g saturated), 71mg cholesterol, 455mg sodium

Pork Chops, Sausage Style

Flavored with the licorice punch of fennel seeds, these chops are like a sausage and pepper sandwich without the bread. Crushing the seeds just before using them helps retain their flavor and fragrance.

PREP: 15 minutes   **GRILL:** 8 to 10 minutes
MAKES: 4 main-dish servings

1	tablespoon fennel seeds
1	garlic clove, crushed with garlic press
1	tablespoon olive oil
¾	teaspoon salt
¾	teaspoon coarsely ground black pepper
4	bone-in pork rib or loin chops, ¾ inch thick (about 6 ounces each), trimmed
2	red and/or yellow peppers, stems and seeds removed, each cut into quarters
4	plum tomatoes, each cut lengthwise in half

1. Prepare outdoor grill for covered direct grilling over medium heat.

2. In mortar with pestle or in zip-tight plastic bag with rolling pin, crush fennel seeds. In cup, mix fennel with garlic, olive oil, and ¹/₂ teaspoon each salt and pepper; use to rub both sides of pork chops. Sprinkle cut sides of peppers and tomatoes with remaining ¹/₄ teaspoon each salt and pepper.

3. Arrange chops and peppers on hot grill rack; cover and cook 5 minutes. Turn chops and peppers over; add tomatoes, cut sides down. Cover and cook until chops are browned outside and still slightly pink in center and vegetables are tender, 3 to 5 minutes.

EACH SERVING: About 315 calories, 25g protein, 10g carbohydrate, 19g total fat (6g saturated), 70mg cholesterol, 490mg sodium

Cuban Pork and Plantains with Black-Bean Salsa

Rub the meat with a peppery garlic coating and grill with plantains for a savory splurge. Make sure the plantains are very ripe: The skin should be black, and the fruit should yield to gentle pressure. (To aid ripening, place in a brown paper bag with a lime.)

PREP: 45 minutes   **GRILL:** 15 to 20 minutes
MAKES: 6 main-dish servings

BLACK-BEAN SALSA

2	limes
1	orange
1	can (15 to 19 ounces) black beans, rinsed and drained
½	small sweet onion, diced
¼	cup loosely packed fresh cilantro leaves, chopped
1	medium jalapeño chile, seeded and minced
¾	teaspoon salt

PORK AND PLANTAINS

2	large garlic cloves, crushed with garlic press
1	teaspoon salt
1½	teaspoons coarsely ground black pepper
2	tablespoons olive oil
2	pork tenderloins (about 12 ounces each), trimmed
3	ripe medium plantains (about 1½ pounds total), each peeled and cut lengthwise in half

1. Prepare salsa: From limes, grate ½ teaspoon peel and squeeze 3 tablespoons juice. From orange, grate ½ teaspoon peel. With knife, remove remaining peel and white pith from orange and cut sections into ½-inch chunks. In medium bowl, combine lime peel and juice, orange peel and chunks, beans, onion, cilantro, jalapeño, and salt. Cover and refrigerate salsa up to 2 days if desired. Makes about 3 cups.

2. Prepare outdoor grill for direct grilling over medium heat.

3. Prepare pork and plantains: In cup, mix garlic, salt, pepper, and 1 tablespoon oil. Rub on pork. Brush plantains with remaining oil.

4. Place tenderloins on hot grill rack and grill 15 to 20 minutes, turning over once, until browned outside and slightly pink in center; an instant-read meat thermometer inserted in thickest part of meat should read 150°F. Place plantains on grill rack and cook, turning once, until tender and browned, 7 to 8 minutes.

5. Transfer plantains to platter. Transfer tenderloins to cutting board; let stand 5 minutes to allow juices to set for easier slicing, then thinly slice. Serve with Black-Bean Salsa.

EACH SERVING PORK AND PLANTAINS: About 315 calories, 28g protein, 29g carbohydrate, 11g total fat (3g saturated), 78mg cholesterol, 440mg sodium

EACH ½ CUP SALSA: About 70 calories, 4g protein, 17g carbohydrate, 0g total fat, 0mg cholesterol, 475mg sodium

Chipotle Pork Chops with Corn Salad

Chipotle pepper sauce is made with chipotle chiles, which are smoked jalapeños. If you don't like the smokiness, you can use your favorite hot pepper sauce.

PREP: 15 minutes   **GRILL:** 8 to 10 minutes
MAKES: 4 main-dish servings

1	tablespoon chipotle pepper sauce
1	teaspoon ground cumin
1	teaspoon olive oil
1	clove garlic, crushed with garlic press
½	teaspoon salt
4	bone-in pork loin or rib chops, ¾ inch thick (8 ounces each), trimmed
3	medium ears corn, husks and silk removed
2	ripe medium tomatoes (6 to 8 ounces each), chopped
½	ripe avocado, peeled, pitted, and cut into ¼-inch pieces
¼	cup loosely packed fresh cilantro leaves, chopped
2	tablespoons fresh lime juice

1. Prepare outdoor grill for covered direct grilling over medium heat.

2. In cup, combine chipotle sauce, cumin, oil, garlic, and ¼ teaspoon salt. Rub an even coating of spice mixture on both sides of pork chops.

3. Place pork chops on hot grill rack. Cover grill and cook until nicely browned on outside and still slightly pink in center, 8 to 10 minutes, turning over once.

4. Meanwhile, cut kernels from corn and transfer to medium bowl. Add tomatoes, avocado, cilantro, lime juice, and remaining ¼ teaspoon salt; stir to combine. Makes about 3 cups.

5. Serve corn salad with grilled pork chops.

EACH SERVING PORK: About 455 calories, 35g protein, 1g carbohydrate, 32g total fat (11g saturated), 106mg cholesterol, 235mg sodium

EACH ¼ CUP CORN SALAD: about 35 calories, 1g protein, 6g carbohydrate, 2g total fat (0g saturated), 0mg cholesterol, 55mg sodium

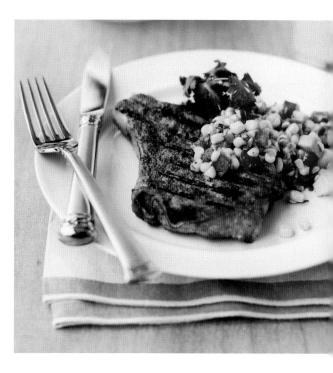

Fennel-Orange Pork Chops with Grilled Vegetables

The combination of fennel, thyme, and orange peel marries well with the richness of pork. Radicchio and Belgian endive, with their slightly bitter taste, also serve as a counterbalance.

PREP: 15 minutes   GRILL: 10 to 12 minutes
MAKES: 4 main-dish servings

1   teaspoon fennel seeds
½   teaspoon dried thyme
¼   teaspoon coarsely ground black pepper
¾   teaspoon salt
1   teaspoon freshly grated orange peel
4   pork rib or loin chops, 1 inch thick (about 6 ounces each), trimmed
1   tablespoon olive oil
1   tablespoon balsamic vinegar
2   heads radicchio di Treviso (about 4 ounces each), each cut lengthwise in half, or 1 large round head radicchio (about 8 ounces), cut into 8 wedges
2   large heads Belgian endive (about 5 ounces each), each cut lengthwise into quarters

1. Prepare outdoor grill for direct grilling over medium heat.

2. In mortar with pestle or in zip-tight plastic bag with rolling pin, crush fennel seeds with thyme, pepper, and ½ teaspoon salt. Stir orange peel into fennel-seed mixture. With hand, rub both sides of pork chops with spice mixture.

3. In medium bowl, mix oil, vinegar, and remaining ¼ teaspoon salt. Add radicchio and endive to bowl and gently toss to coat.

4. Place pork chops on hot grill rack and grill 5 minutes. Turn chops and add vegetables to grill. Grill until chops have just a hint of pink color in center and vegetables are browned, 5 to 7 minutes longer.

5. Serve pork chops with grilled vegetables.

EACH SERVING: About 690 calories, 37g protein, 38g carbohydrate, 43g total fat (16g saturated), 172mg cholesterol, 860mg sodium

Baby Back Ribs Supreme

Only fifteen minutes of grilling time! The trick? Steam the seasoned ribs for an hour in the oven up to two days before barbecuing. With both the ribs and the BBQ sauce prepared in advance, this could easily become a part of your summer weeknight repertoire.

PREP: **1 hour 15 minutes**   GRILL: **15 minutes**
MAKES: **8 main-dish servings**

4	teaspoons grated, peeled fresh ginger
2	teaspoons freshly grated lemon peel
¾	teaspoon salt
2	garlic cloves, crushed with garlic press
4	racks pork baby back ribs (about 1 pound each; see Tip)
2	cups boiling water
2	cups Secret-Recipe BBQ Sauce (page 134)

1. Preheat oven to 350°F. In cup, mix ginger, lemon peel, salt, and garlic until combined. Rub ginger mixture on ribs.

2. Place ribs in large roasting pan (15 ½″ by 11 ½″), overlapping slightly. Pour *boiling water* into roasting pan. Cover pan tightly with foil and place in oven. Steam ribs 1 hour.

3. Meanwhile, prepare Secret-Recipe BBQ Sauce.

4. Carefully remove foil from roasting pan (escaping steam is very hot). Remove ribs from pan; discard water. Ribs may be grilled immediately or refrigerated, covered, up to 2 days before grilling.

5. Prepare outdoor grill for direct grilling over medium heat.

6. Place ribs, meat side up, on hot grill rack; grill 5 minutes, turning over once. Turn ribs again; brush with BBQ sauce and grill 5 minutes. Repeat turning and brushing once more. Cut racks into 2-rib portions; serve with remaining BBQ sauce.

EACH SERVING: About 460 calories, 27g protein, 12g carbohydrate, 33g total fat (12g saturated), 129mg cholesterol, 570mg sodium

> **TIP:** When buying baby backs, look for ribs that are meaty, with a minimum of visible fat.

Sausage and Pepper Grill

Grill Italian hard rolls and serve the sausage and peppers on top for a hearty open-faced sandwich reminiscent of those found at street fairs. If you'd prefer, toss the grilled sausages and vegetables with a bowl of cooked ziti, add grated Parmesan cheese, and serve.

PREP: 15 minutes   **GRILL:** 15 to 20 minutes
MAKES: 4 main-dish servings

⅓ cup balsamic vinegar

1 teaspoon brown sugar

½ teaspoon salt

¼ teaspoon coarsely ground black pepper

2 medium red peppers, stems and seeds removed, cut into 1½-inch-wide strips

2 medium green peppers, stems and seeds removed, cut into 1½-inch-wide strips

2 large red onions (12 ounces each), each cut into 6 wedges

1 tablespoon olive oil

¾ pound sweet Italian sausage links

¾ pound hot Italian sausage links

1. Prepare outdoor grill for direct grilling over medium heat.

2. In cup, with fork, mix balsamic vinegar, brown sugar, salt, and black pepper (see Tip). In large bowl, toss red and green peppers and onions with oil to coat.

3. Place sausages on hot grill rack and grill until golden brown and cooked through, 15 to 20 minutes, turning occasionally. Place vegetables on grill at same time as sausages, turning occasionally and brushing with balsamic mixture during last 3 minutes of cooking, until tender, about 15 minutes. Transfer vegetables and sausages to platter as they finish cooking.

4. To serve, cut sausages diagonally into 2-inch slices. Drizzle remaining balsamic mixture over vegetables.

EACH SERVING: About 500 calories, 27g protein, 19g carbohydrate, 36g total fat (12g saturated), 97mg cholesterol, 1,450mg sodium

> **TIP:** Adding a small amount of brown sugar to ordinary balsamic vinegar gives it a smooth, mellow flavor similar to that of an aged vinegar. Try this trick the next time you make a balsamic vinegar dressing.

Spiced Kielbasa and Summer Fruit Kabobs

Smoky sausage and sweet fruit are a delicious combination. To keep grill time short, check out the fully-cooked sausages now available. Flavors range from Chicken & Apple to Sweet Basil and Roasted Garlic. You can also use nectarines or pears in place of the other fruit.

PREP: 10 minutes   **GRILL:** 6 to 7 minutes

MAKES: 4 main-dish servings

1   package (16 ounces) light kielbasa or other fully cooked smoked sausage, cut into 1-inch chunks

3   apricots, each pitted and cut into quarters

2   ripe plums or peaches, pitted and cut into 1-inch chunks

4 to 6 (12-inch) metal skewers

3   tablespoons sweet orange marmalade

1   tablespoon Chinese five-spice powder

1. Prepare outdoor grill for covered direct grilling over medium heat.

2. Meanwhile, alternately thread kielbasa, apricots, and plums onto skewers. In cup, combine marmalade and five-spice powder.

3. Place skewers on hot grill rack. Cover grill and cook until kielbasa browns and fruit chars slightly, about 5 minutes, turning skewers occasionally. Uncover grill. Brush marmalade mixture all over kielbasa and fruit. Cook 1 to 2 minutes longer, turning occasionally.

EACH SERVING: About 340 calories, 17g protein, 22g carbohydrate, 22g total fat (8g saturated), 76mg cholesterol, 1,032mg sodium

Fish and Shellfish

Eating fish is a good way to add heart-healthy omega-3 fatty acids to your diet, and grilling fish (outside or in a grill pan) is a fantastic way to enjoy this good-for-you protein. Lots of different types of fish work well on the grill, including halibut, catfish, salmon, snapper, and tuna. Our recipe selection shows a wide range of flavor possibilities, from Thai Snapper to Pan-Grilled Catfish to Jerk Halibut Steaks.

Shrimp and scallops seem to be made for the grill, perfect mouthfuls with crispy smoked edges, served up on easy-to cook skewers. We've got tasty recipes to choose from, including Five-Spice Shrimp and Scallops and Shrimp and Scallops Kabobs. And for something a little different, try our Garlicky Grilled Clams and Mussels or Grilled Squid and Peppers with Arugula.

Shrimp with Asian Barbecue Sauce, page 117

Grilled Halibut with Fresh Dill

If halibut is not available, substitute swordfish or tuna steaks. White-wine Worcestershire sauce is particularly good with seafood and poultry. If you can't find it, use 2 tablespoons original Worcestershire mixed with 2 tablespoons water.

PREP: **5 minutes plus marinating**
GRILL: **about 10 minutes**
MAKES: **4 main-dish servings**

¼ cup white-wine Worcestershire sauce
2 tablespoons fresh lemon juice
1 tablespoon olive oil
1 tablespoon minced fresh dill
¼ teaspoon coarsely ground black pepper
2 large halibut steaks, 1 inch thick (about 12 ounces each)

1. In medium bowl, stir Worcestershire, lemon juice, oil, dill, and pepper. Place halibut in large zip-tight plastic bag. Add marinade. Seal bag, pressing out excess air, and place on plate; refrigerate up to 2 hours, turning once.

2. Prepare outdoor grill for direct grilling over low heat.

3. Place halibut on hot grill rack, reserving marinade. Grill halibut, turning occasionally and basting frequently with reserved marinade, until opaque throughout, about 10 minutes.

EACH SERVING: About 195 calories, 29g protein, 3g carbohydrate, 7g total fat (1g saturated), 45mg cholesterol, 200mg sodium

Greek-Style Grilled Halibut

Greek cooks have long favored the clean, simple flavors of fresh lemon and oregano with fish. One bite of this, and you'll understand why.

PREP: **10 minutes plus marinating**
GRILL: **6 to 8 minutes**
MAKES: **4 main-dish servings**

1 lemon
3 tablespoons olive oil
2 garlic cloves, finely chopped
2 teaspoons chopped fresh oregano
½ teaspoon salt
4 small halibut steaks, ¾ inch thick (about 6 ounces each)

1. From lemon, grate 1 teaspoon peel and squeeze 2 tablespoons juice. In large bowl, with wire whisk, whisk lemon peel and juice, oil, garlic, oregano, and salt until mixed. Add halibut steaks, turning each to coat. Cover and refrigerate 1 hour to marinate, turning once or twice.

2. Meanwhile, prepare outdoor grill for covered direct grilling over medium heat.

3. Remove halibut from bowl, reserving marinade. Place halibut on hot grill rack and cook, brushing with marinade during first half of grilling, until halibut is just opaque throughout, 6 to 8 minutes, turning over once.

EACH SERVING: About 199 calories, 29g protein, 1g carbohydrate, 8g total fat (1g saturated), 44mg cholesterol, 218mg sodium

Jerk Halibut Steaks with Sweet Potato Wedges

Halibut, a firm-fleshed fish, is often sold as fillets, but it's one of the few flat fish thick enough to be cut into steaks—which are usually a better buy.

PREP: 15 minutes **GRILL:** 8 to 10 minutes
MAKES: 4 main-dish servings

2	pounds sweet potatoes (about 2 large)
2	green onions, chopped
1	jalapeño chile, seeded and chopped
2	tablespoons fresh lime juice
2	tablespoons Worcestershire sauce
1	tablespoon peeled, grated fresh ginger
1	teaspoon dried thyme
1	teaspoon ground allspice
2	tablespoons olive oil
¼	teaspoon plus ⅛ teaspoon ground red pepper (cayenne)
½	teaspoon salt
4	small halibut steaks, 1 inch thick (about 6 ounces each)

lime wedges for garnish

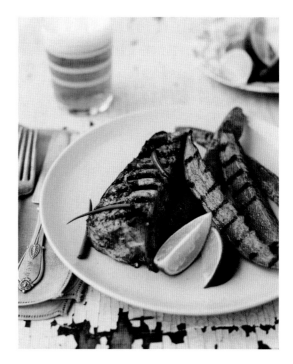

1. Lightly grease grill rack. Prepare outdoor grill for covered direct grilling over medium heat.

2. Cut each unpeeled sweet potato lengthwise in half. Place sweet potato halves on microwave-safe plate and cook in microwave oven on High 8 minutes or until almost fork-tender, rearranging sweet potatoes halfway through cooking.

3. Meanwhile, in bowl, combine green onions, jalapeño, lime juice, Worcestershire, ginger, thyme, allspice, 1 tablespoon oil, ¼ teaspoon ground red pepper, and ¼ teaspoon salt. Add halibut, turning to coat. Let stand 5 minutes.

4. Cut each sweet potato half into 4 wedges. In another medium bowl, toss sweet potatoes with remaining ¼ teaspoon salt, 1 tablespoon oil, and ⅛ teaspoon ground red pepper until coated.

5. Place halibut and sweet potatoes on hot grill rack. Spoon half of jerk sauce remaining in marinating bowl on halibut; discard remainder. Grill halibut steaks until opaque throughout, 8 to 10 minutes, turning over once. Grill sweet potato wedges until tender and lightly charred, 6 to 7 minutes, turning over once. Transfer to platter as they are done. Garnish with lime wedges.

EACH SERVING: About 410 calories, 38g protein, 42g carbohydrate, 9g total fat (1g saturated), 54mg cholesterol, 390mg sodium

Pan-Grilled Catfish with Tomato-Chipotle Salsa over Polenta

Polenta is made from finely ground yellow cornmeal. We make this side dish with low-fat milk and chicken broth to keep it light.

PREP: 30 minutes   GRILL: 20 minutes
MAKES: 4 main-dish servings

4	large plum tomatoes (about 1 pound total), each cut lengthwise in half
1	small red onion, cut crosswise into ½-inch-thick slices
	nonstick cooking spray
4	catfish fillets (6 ounces each)
¾	teaspoon chipotle chile powder
¾	teaspoon salt
3	cups low-fat (1%) milk
1	can (14 to 14½ ounces) reduced-sodium chicken broth (1¾ cups)
¾	cup instant polenta
1	cup fresh corn kernels (from 2 ears corn) or 1 cup frozen (thawed) corn kernels
2	teaspoons fresh lime juice

1. Preheat large ridged grill pan over medium-high heat. On sheet of waxed paper, place tomato halves and onion slices. Spray on both sides with cooking spray, place on grill pan, and cook until lightly browned and softened, 10 minutes, turning once. Transfer to cutting board.

2. While tomatoes and onion are cooking, place catfish fillets on same waxed paper. Sprinkle with ½ teaspoon chipotle chile powder and ¼ teaspoon salt to season both sides, then spray both sides with cooking spray.

3. Place catfish on grill pan; cook just until it turns opaque throughout, 7 to 8 minutes, turning over once.

4. Meanwhile, prepare polenta: In 3-quart saucepan, combine milk, broth, and ¼ teaspoon salt; cover and heat to boiling over high heat. Remove cover; slowly whisk in polenta and cook, stirring, until mixture begins to thicken. Reduce heat to low; cover and simmer 5 minutes, stirring occasionally. Stir in corn. Remove from heat.

5. Coarsely chop grilled tomatoes and onion; transfer, with any juices, to medium bowl. Stir in lime juice and remaining ¼ teaspoon chipotle chile powder and ¼ teaspoon salt. Makes about 1¾ cups.

6. To serve, divide polenta among 4 dinner plates; top with grilled catfish and tomato-chipotle salsa.

EACH SERVING: About 480 calories, 38g protein, 46g carbohydrate, 16g total fat (4g saturated), 87mg cholesterol, 980mg sodium

Thai Snapper

Tender fillets are seasoned with lime and ginger and cooked in a foil packet. Don't be tempted to assemble the packets too far ahead of time; the lime juice will start to "cook" the fillets, giving them a mushy texture. Instead, cut the vegetables and prepare the lime juice mixture several hours early and assemble the packets just before cooking.

PREP: 30 minutes   GRILL: 8 minutes
MAKES: 4 main-dish servings

3   tablespoons fresh lime juice
1   tablespoon Asian fish sauce
1   tablespoon olive oil
1   teaspoon grated, peeled fresh ginger (see Tip)
½   teaspoon sugar
½   teaspoon minced garlic
4   (16" by 12") heavy-duty foil sheets
4   red snapper fillets (about 6 ounces each)
1   large carrot, peeled and cut into 2¼-inch-long matchstick strips
1   large green onion, thinly sliced
¼   cup loosely packed fresh cilantro leaves

1. Prepare outdoor grill for direct grilling over medium heat.

2. In small bowl, mix lime juice, fish sauce, oil, ginger, sugar, and garlic.

3. Fold each foil sheet crosswise in half and open up again. Place 1 fillet, skin side down, on one half of each foil sheet. Top each with carrot strips, green onion, and cilantro. Spoon lime juice mixture over snapper and vegetables. Fold unfilled half of foil over fish. To seal packets, beginning at a corner where foil is folded, make small ½-inch folds, with each new fold overlapping previous one, until packet is completely sealed. Packet will resemble half-circle.

4. Place packets on hot grill rack and cook 8 minutes.

5. To serve, with kitchen shears, cut an X in top of each packet to allow steam to escape before carefully opening foil.

EACH SERVING: About 230 calories, 36g protein, 5g carbohydrate, 6g total fat (1g saturated), 63mg cholesterol, 270mg sodium

TIP: Use a spoon, not a vegetable peeler, next time you need peeled ginger. Use its edge or tip to scrape away the skin. You'll find that a spoon maneuvers better than a peeler around the rhizome's knobby ends. It also removes a thinner layer of skin, keeping more of the ginger for you to use.

Everything You Need to Know about Buying and Storing Fish

BUYING

■ Shop in a clean, reputable market. Don't buy fish that has a distinct "fishy" odor (fresh fish smells like a sea breeze).

■ Buying frozen fish? Select a brand that's well wrapped and rock hard, without any freezer burn.

■ When buying a whole fish, plan on 1/2 to 3/4 pound per person; purchase 1/3 to 1/2 pound per person for fillets and steaks.

■ Make sure fillets and steaks have a shiny, moist, translucent appearance; the flesh should be firm with no gaps between the flakes. There should be no browning or drying around the edges and no evidence of extra liquid.

■ If you're purchasing a whole fish, check to see if it has bright, shiny eyes and scales; the scales should cling tightly to the skin.

STORING

■ Make the fish market your last stop before heading home. To be extra safe on extended rides or on hot days, store fish in a small cooler with a couple of ice packs.

■ Store fish in the coldest part of the fridge— either at the back of the bottom shelf or in the meat drawer.

■ Always keep raw seafood away from other foods to avoid cross-contamination, and wash hands and surfaces thoroughly with hot soapy water after handling.

■ Plan to use fresh fish right away or, at the very latest, within a day or two. Frozen fish can be kept up to six months.

■ If you need to keep fish overnight, remove it from the packaging and pat dry. Then cover it loosely with plastic wrap and layer the wrapped fish with ice in a colander placed over a bowl to catch drips.

Mediterranean Grilled Sea Bass

Grilled whole fish is a summer favorite in the Mediterranean. Sea bass is lovely on the grill; its firm white flesh holds up very well. If you can't get sea bass, substitute red snapper or striped bass.

PREP: 10 minutes plus marinating
GRILL: 12 to 14 minutes
MAKES: 4 main-dish servings

2	lemons
3	tablespoons olive oil
1	tablespoon chopped fresh oregano
1	teaspoon ground coriander
1¼	teaspoons salt
2	whole sea bass, cleaned and scaled (about 1½ pounds each)
¼	teaspoon ground black pepper
2	large oregano sprigs

1. Prepare outdoor grill for covered direct grilling over medium heat.

2. Meanwhile, from 1 lemon, grate 1 tablespoon peel and squeeze 2 tablespoons juice. Cut one half of remaining lemon into slices; cut the remaining half into wedges to use for serving. In small bowl, stir lemon juice and peel, oil, chopped oregano, coriander, and ¼ teaspoon salt.

3. Rinse fish and pat dry with paper towels. Make 3 diagonal slashes in both sides of each fish. Sprinkle inside and out with pepper and remaining 1 teaspoon salt. Place lemon slices and oregano sprigs inside fish cavities. Place fish in 13" by 9" glass baking dish. Set aside half of oil mixture. Rub remaining half of oil mixture on outside of both fish. Let stand 15 minutes at room temperature.

4. Place fish on hot grill rack. Cover grill and cook fish until just opaque throughout, 12 to 14 minutes, turning over once.

5. To serve, place fish on cutting board. Working with one fish at a time, with knife, cut along backbone from head to tail. Slide wide metal spatula or cake server under front section of top fillet and lift off from backbone; transfer to platter. Gently pull out backbone and rib bones from bottom fillet and discard. Transfer bottom fillet to platter. Repeat with second fish. Drizzle fillets with remaining oil mixture. Serve with reserved lemon wedges.

EACH SERVING: About 305 calories, 40g protein, 1g carbohydrate, 15g total fat (3g saturated), 90mg cholesterol, 730mg sodium

Salmon Teriyaki

For an easy accompaniment, throw some whole green onions on the grill alongside the salmon. They'll cook in a few minutes; turn often.

PREP: 10 minutes   **GRILL:** about 8 minutes
MAKES: 4 main-dish servings

6	tablespoons teriyaki sauce
1	tablespoon brown sugar
1	teaspoon Asian sesame oil
4	salmon steaks, ¾ inch thick (about 6 ounces each)
1	green onion, thinly sliced on diagonal

1. Prepare outdoor grill for covered direct grilling over medium heat.

2. Meanwhile, in 2-quart saucepan, heat teriyaki sauce, brown sugar, and sesame oil to boiling over medium-high heat. Boil until slightly thickened, about 3 minutes.

3. With tweezers, remove any pin bones from salmon. Place salmon on hot grill rack. Cover grill and cook salmon, turning once and brushing frequently with teriyaki mixture, until just opaque throughout, about 8 minutes.

4. Transfer salmon steaks to platter; sprinkle with green onion.

EACH SERVING: About 320 calories, 36g protein, 8g carbohydrate, 15g total fat (3g saturated), 110mg cholesterol, 1,120mg sodium

Everything You Need to Know about Preparing Fish

■ **Defrosting:** To ensure the best texture and minimize the growth of bacteria, defrost frozen fish as slowly as possible, preferably in the refrigerator on a plate for approximately 24 hours. If you're in a hurry, place well-wrapped fish in a bowl of cold water. Change the water every 30 minutes until the fish is defrosted (1 to 2 hours per pound of seafood). Be sure to cook immediately.

■ **Removing pin bones:** Although often sold as boneless, some fillets may still have tiny bones near the head end as well as a row of bones down the center of a fillet. You can feel for these small bones by running your fingers along the fillet. They are easily removed with tweezers or needle-nose pliers.

■ **Skinning:** The skin of most fish is edible (and delicious when cooked to a crisp!), but you can easily skin a fillet if necessary. Place the fillet skin side down with the narrow end near you. At the edge of the narrow end, make a small cut through flesh to skin. Grab the skin and slip the knife blade between it and the fillet and, holding the blade amost parallel to work surface, use a gentle sawing motion to separate the skin from the flesh all the way to the head end.

Spiced Salmon Steaks

Juicy summer-ripe red and yellow tomatoes are a cool and easy go-along for this entrée. Dress the tomatoes with a fruity olive oil and a sprinkling of finely shredded basil. Try this preparation with thick bluefish fillets, too; the spice mixture is a delicious complement to the richness of the fish.

PREP: **10 minutes**   GRILL: **about 8 minutes**

MAKES: **4 main-dish servings**

1	tablespoon chili powder
2	teaspoons light brown sugar
1	teaspoon ground cumin
1	teaspoon dried thyme
1	teaspoon salt
2	teaspoons olive oil
4	large salmon steaks, ¾ inch thick (about 8 ounces each)

lemon wedges (optional)

1. Prepare outdoor grill for direct grilling over medium heat.

2. In cup, mix chili powder, brown sugar, cumin, thyme, salt, and oil.

3. With tweezers, remove any pin bones from salmon. With hands, rub spice mixture on both sides of salmon steaks.

4. Place salmon on hot grill rack. Grill, turning once, until just opaque throughout, about 8 minutes. Serve with lemon wedges, if you like.

EACH SERVING: About 405 calories, 40g protein, 4g carbohydrate, 24g total fat (5g saturated), 118mg cholesterol, 720mg sodium

> **TIP:** This recipe doubles easily. Prepare a double batch, serve half, and refrigerate the remainder. Serve the salmon chilled or at room temperature the next day.

STEAK OR FILLET?

A steak is a cross-section cut containing a portion of the fish's backbone and possibly a few rib bones; a fillet is a boneless section of flesh cut from either side of the fish. Salmon steaks and fillets are equally tasty and are interchangeable in most recipes. However, diners afraid of bones may prefer fillets.

Grilled Salmon with Herb-Caper Cream

A grill pan cooks simply seasoned salmon steaks perfectly. All you need is our light yet flavorful sauce, made in a mini food processor, to top it off. Add a few whole green onions to the pan and grill them alongside the salmon for a delicious edible garnish.

PREP: 5 minutes   GRILL: about 8 minutes

MAKES: 4 main-dish servings

4   salmon steaks, ¾ inch thick
     (about 6 ounces each)
½   teaspoon salt
½   teaspoon coarsely ground black pepper
½   cup loosely packed fresh parsley leaves
2   tablespoons capers, drained
1   green onion, cut into 4 pieces
⅓   cup reduced-fat sour cream
¼   cup light mayonnaise
1   tablespoon fresh lemon juice

1. Grease ridged grill pan; heat over medium heat until very hot but not smoking. Sprinkle salmon with salt and ¼ teaspoon pepper, and place in grill pan. Cook until salmon flakes easily when tested with a fork, about 8 minutes, turning once; transfer to platter.

2. Meanwhile, in mini food processor, with sharp side of blade facing up, process parsley, capers, and green onion until finely chopped. Transfer mixture to small bowl and stir in sour cream, mayonnaise, lemon juice, and remaining ¼ teaspoon pepper until blended. Makes about ¾ cup sauce.

3. Serve sauce with salmon.

EACH SERVING SALMON: About 230 calories, 32g protein, 0g carbohydrate, 10g total fat (2g saturated), 91mg cholesterol, 360mg sodium

EACH TABLESPOON SAUCE: About 30 calories, 0g protein, 1g carbohydrate, 3g total fat (1g saturated), 4mg cholesterol, 85mg sodium

FARM-RAISED VERSUS WILD SALMON

Farm-raised (usually Atlantic) salmon, with a rich, almost buttery texture and a milder flavor than its wilder sister, is mainly bred along the northeast coast of the United States or off the coast of Chile, first in freshwater hatcheries and then in pens submerged in cold saltwater off the coastline, where the fish have a chance to swim against currents and changing tides. Since it's available all year, we generally use it in our recipes.

Wild salmon, with a lean, firm texture and a more pronounced fish flavor, comes mostly from Alaska and is available only in summer months unless purchased frozen or canned. Alaska salmon is called "wild" because the fish swim freely in the Bering Sea, the Gulf of Alaska, and the waters of the northern Pacific. The five commercially sold varieties of wild Alaskan salmon are King (or Chinook), Sockeye (or Red or Blueback), Silver (or Coho), Chum, and Pink (which is primarily canned).

Spiced Grilled Tuna on Spinach Salad

A blend of aromatic spices rubbed on tuna steaks before pan-grilling adds great flavor.

PREP: 25 minutes   GRILL: 8 to 10 minutes
MAKES: 4 main-dish servings

TUNA WITH SPICE RUB

1	tablespoon olive oil
1	teaspoon ground cumin
1	teaspoon ground coriander
1	teaspoon paprika
1	teaspoon freshly grated lime peel
3/4	teaspoon salt
1/2	teaspoon coarsely ground black pepper
4	tuna steaks, 1 inch thick (about 6 ounces each)

SPINACH SALAD

2	tablespoons olive oil
2	tablespoons fresh lime juice
1	teaspoon sugar
1/4	teaspoon ground cumin
1/4	teaspoon salt
1/8	teaspoon coarsely ground black pepper
1	bag (6 ounces) baby spinach
1/2	English (seedless) cucumber (about 8 ounces), unpeeled, cut lengthwise in half, then thinly sliced crosswise
1	bunch radishes, each cut in half, then thinly sliced
4	radishes with tops for garnish

1. Prepare spice rub: In small bowl, with spoon, combine oil, cumin, coriander, paprika, lime peel, salt, and pepper until well blended. Rub spice mixture on both sides of tuna steaks.

2. Heat ridged grill pan over medium heat until hot but not smoking. Add tuna to pan and cook 8 to 10 minutes, until fish turns opaque through-out, turning over once. (If you prefer seared tuna, grill about 2 minutes per side.) Transfer to cutting board.

3. Meanwhile, prepare salad: In large bowl, with wire whisk or fork, mix oil, lime juice, sugar, cumin, salt, and pepper. Add cucumber, spinach, and sliced radishes; toss to coat.

4. Cut tuna steaks into 1/2-inch-thick slices. Arrange salad on dinner plates or large platter; top with steak. Garnish with radishes.

EACH SERVING: About 300 calories, 42g protein, 5g carbohydrate, 12g total fat (2g saturated), 76mg cholesterol, 700 mg sodium

Shrimp with Asian Barbecue Sauce

Fresh ginger and five spice powder create a delicious sauce for these succulent shrimp kabobs. Serve on a bed of romaine with extra sauce for dipping. For photo, see page 104.

PREP: 15 minutes   GRILL: 3 to 4 minutes
MAKES: 4 main-dish servings

romaine lettuce leaves
1¼ pounds large shrimp
4   (10- to 12-inch) skewers
⅓   cup hoisin sauce
3   tablespoons ketchup
1½ teaspoons grated, peeled fresh ginger
¼   teaspoon Chinese five-spice powder
2   tablespoons rice vinegar
2   tablespoons water

1. Soak skewers in hot water at least 20 minutes. Lightly grease grill rack. Prepare outdoor grill for direct grilling over medium heat.

2. Arrange romaine on platter and set aside. Shell and devein shrimp, leaving tail shell on, if you like. Thread shrimp on skewers.

3. In small bowl, stir hoisin sauce, ketchup, ginger, five-spice powder, and 1 tablespoon vinegar. Transfer ¼ cup sauce to ramekin; stir in water and remaining 1 tablespoon vinegar and reserve to use as dipping sauce.

4. Brush shrimp with some barbecue sauce remaining in bowl. Place shrimp on hot grill rack and cook 2 minutes. Brush with more sauce; turn, brush with remaining sauce, and grill until shrimp turn opaque throughout, 1 to 2 minutes longer.

5. Arrange shrimp skewers on romaine and serve with reserved dipping sauce.

EACH SERVING: About 185 calories, 25g protein, 13g carbohydrate, 3g total fat (1g saturated), 175mg cholesterol, 540mg sodium

---

SHELLING AND DEVEINING SHRIMP

Deveining small and medium shrimp is optional. However, do remove the vein of large shrimp; it can contain grit.

1. With kitchen shears or small knife, cut the shrimp shell along the outer curve, just deep enough into the flesh to expose the dark vein.

2. Peel back the shell from the cut and gently separate the shell from the shrimp. Discard the shell (or use it to make stock).

3. Hold the shrimp under cold running water; remove the vein with the tip of the knife.

Five-Spice Shrimp and Scallops

An intriguing mix of sweet and spicy flavors. Great with our Cucumber Relish (page 137).

PREP: 20 minutes   GRILL: 4 to 5 minutes
MAKES: 6 main-dish servings

1   pound large shrimp
¾   pound sea scallops
1   tablespoon light brown sugar
1   tablespoon soy sauce
1   tablespoon vegetable oil
2   teaspoons Chinese five-spice powder
1¼ teaspoons salt
¼   teaspoon coarsely ground black pepper
6   (12-inch) metal skewers

1. Prepare outdoor grill for direct grilling over medium heat. Shell and devein shrimp, leaving tail shell on, if you like; rinse with cold water. Pull off and discard tough crescent-shaped muscle, if any, from each scallop. Rinse well to remove sand from crevices. Pat shrimp and scallops dry with paper towels.

2. In large bowl, mix brown sugar, soy sauce, oil, five-spice powder, salt, and pepper; add shrimp and scallops, tossing to coat.

3. Onto skewers, alternately thread shrimp and scallops. Place on hot grill rack; cook until shrimp and scallops turn opaque throughout, 4 to 5 minutes, turning occasionally and dabbing with any remaining spice mixture halfway through cooking.

EACH SERVING: About 155 calories, 26g protein, 4g carbohydrate, 4g total fat (0g saturated), 150mg cholesterol, 905mg sodium

Scallop and Cherry Tomato Skewers

These skewers make for a memorable contrast in flavor and texture—the smooth creaminess of the scallops against the burst of juice from the sweet and slightly tart grilled tomatoes.

PREP: 10 minutes   GRILL: 12 to 14 minutes
MAKES: 4 main-dish servings

8   (8-inch) bamboo skewers
1   lemon
2   tablespoons olive oil
2   tablespoons Dijon mustard
⅛   teaspoon salt
24   cherry tomatoes
16   large sea scallops (1¼ pounds)

1. Soak skewers in hot water at least 20 minutes. Prepare outdoor grill for direct grilling over medium heat.

2. Meanwhile, from lemon, grate 1½ teaspoons peel and squeeze 1 tablespoon juice. In small bowl, whisk lemon peel and juice, oil, Dijon, and salt until blended; set aside.

3. Thread 3 tomatoes and 2 scallops alternately on each skewer, beginning and ending with tomatoes.

4. Brush scallops and tomatoes with half of Dijon mixture; place on hot grill rack. Cook 7 to 9 minutes, turning several times. Brush with remaining Dijon mixture, and cook until scallops just turn opaque throughout, about 5 minutes longer.

EACH SERVING: About 215 calories, 25g protein, 9g carbohydrate, 9g total fat (1g saturated), 47mg cholesterol, 355mg sodium

Shrimp and Scallop Kabobs

Shrimp and scallops cook in a flash and require no marinating. If the scallops are very large, halve them horizontally. Don't substitute bay scallops; they're small and will cook too quickly. If you like, serve with Pineapple Salsa (page 136) and a bowl of rice.

PREP: **20 minutes**   GRILL: **4 to 5 minutes**
MAKES: **6 main-dish servings**

1	pound large shrimp
1	pound large sea scallops
3	tablespoons soy sauce
3	tablespoons seasoned rice vinegar
2	tablespoons grated, peeled fresh ginger
1	tablespoon brown sugar
1	tablespoon Asian sesame oil
2	garlic cloves, crushed with garlic press
1	bunch green onions, cut diagonally into 3-inch-long pieces
12	cherry tomatoes
6	(12-inch) metal skewers

1. Prepare outdoor grill for direct grilling over medium heat.

2. Shell and devein shrimp, leaving tail shell on, if you like; rinse with cold water. Pull off and discard tough crescent-shaped muscle, if any, from each scallop. Rinse scallops well to remove sand from crevices. Pat shrimp and scallops dry with paper towels.

3. In large bowl, mix soy sauce, vinegar, ginger, brown sugar, sesame oil, and garlic (see Tip). Add shrimp and scallops; toss until evenly coated.

4. Alternately thread shrimp, scallops, green onions, and tomatoes onto skewers. Place on hot grill rack; grill, turning occasionally and basting with any remaining soy-sauce mixture halfway through cooking, until just opaque throughout, 4 to 5 minutes.

EACH SERVING: About 185 calories, 26g protein, 10g carbohydrate, 4g total fat (1g saturated), 118mg cholesterol, 880mg sodium

> **TIP:** The soy mixture can be made several hours in advance, covered, and refrigerated. Whisk to combine before adding the shrimp and scallops.

BUYING SHRIMP

When purchasing shrimp by the pound, remember that the number you'll get depends on the size you select. Here, the quantity per pound for the different sizes available:

SHRIMP SIZE	NUMBER PER POUND
Small	36–45
Medium	31–35
Large	21–30
Extra large	16–20
Jumbo	11–15

Garlicky Grilled Clams and Mussels

Buy your shellfish from a reputable purveyor and plan to serve them the day of purchase. If you're not cooking right away, store them in a large bowl covered with a wet towel in the refrigerator, not on ice, until the grill is ready.

PREP: 20 minutes   GRILL: about 10 minutes
MAKES: 4 main-dish or 8 appetizer servings

4	tablespoons butter or margarine, cut into pieces
2	tablespoons olive oil
3	garlic cloves, minced
1	large shallot, minced (¼ cup)
½	cup dry white wine
¼	teaspoon crushed red pepper
2	pounds mussels, scrubbed, with beards removed
2	dozen littleneck clams, scrubbed
⅔	cup loosely packed fresh parsley leaves, coarsely chopped

lemon and/or lime wedges

French bread slices

1. Prepare outdoor grill for covered direct grilling over medium-high heat.

2. Place butter and oil in large disposable foil roasting pan (about 16″ by 12 ½″). Place pan on hot grill rack and heat until butter has melted. Remove pan from grill. Add garlic, shallot, wine, and crushed red pepper; stir to combine. Add mussels and clams, spreading out to an even layer. Cover pan tightly with foil.

3. Return pan to grill rack. Cover grill and cook until mussels and clams open, 8 to 10 minutes.

4. Discard any mussels or clams that have not opened. Sprinkle with parsley and serve with lemon and/or lime wedges and French bread.

EACH SERVING: About 360 calories, 28g protein, 10g carbohydrate, 22g total fat (14g saturated), 130mg cholesterol, 408mg sodium

Grilled Squid and Peppers with Arugula

Squid can turn chewy if it's not cooked properly. To ensure a tender result, remove each piece from the grill just as it becomes opaque.

PREP: 15 minutes   **GRILL:** 11 to 17 minutes
MAKES: 4 main-dish servings

1½ pounds cleaned squid

1   garlic clove, crushed with garlic press

2   tablespoons plus 2 teaspoons extra-virgin olive oil

½ teaspoon salt

¼ teaspoon coarsely ground black pepper

4   medium peppers (red, orange, and/or yellow)

2   lemons, each cut in half

1   bag (5 ounces) baby arugula

1. With kitchen shears, cut each squid body lengthwise down 1 side and open flat. Cut large tentacles in half. Rinse squid with cold water and pat dry with paper towels. Transfer squid to bowl; add garlic, 1 tablespoon oil, ¼ teaspoon salt, and pepper, and toss to coat; set aside. Cut each pepper lengthwise into quarters; discard seeds and stems.

2. Heat large ridged grill pan over medium-high heat (or prepare outdoor grill for direct grilling over medium-high heat).

3. In large bowl, toss peppers with 2 teaspoons oil. Place on grill pan and cook until charred and tender, 10 to 15 minutes, turning once. Place lemon halves, cut sides down, on grill with peppers and cook until marks appear and lemons soften, about 5 minutes. Transfer peppers to large bowl. Set lemon halves aside.

4. Place squid on grill pan and cook just until opaque throughout, 1 to 2 minutes, turning over once. Add squid to peppers in bowl and toss with remaining 1 tablespoon oil and ¼ teaspoon salt.

5. Arrange arugula on platter; top with squid mixture. Serve with grilled lemons to squeeze over servings.

EACH SERVING: About 300 calories, 30g protein, 23g carbohydrate, 12g total fat (2g saturated), 396mg cholesterol, 380mg sodium

Vegetables

If you've got the grill going, why not throw some vegetables on there, too? We've provided you with a handy Guide to Grilling Vegetables, with basic directions for grilling everything from corn on the cob to portobello mushrooms and vine-ripe tomatoes to perfection.

Our Grilled Vegetables with Bagna Cauda, Grilled Vegetarian Burritos, and Grilled Vegetable Stacks are hearty enough to serve as a main course if you're looking for a healthier alternative or are entertaining vegetarians, who often have to miss out when attending a barbecue. We've got three delicious ways to grill up corn, including with chili and lime, molasses, and herbs. And our recipes for eggplant, fennel, and tomatoes are sure to be crowd-pleasers, and they complement the meat, fish, and poultry dishes in this book beautifully.

Grilled Eggplant with Feta and Fresh Mint, page 130

Grilled Vegetables with Bagna Cauda

Classic bagna cauda is a sauce made with olive oil, butter, anchovies, and garlic, served warm, as an appetizer, with raw vegetables for dipping. Our version, poured over a platter of grilled vegetables, is hearty enough for a main dish.

PREP: 30 minutes   GRILL: 5 to 15 minutes
MAKES: 10 side-dish servings

BAGNA CAUDA

¼   cup olive oil
5   canned anchovy fillets, minced
2   garlic cloves, minced
½   teaspoon freshly grated lemon peel
½   teaspoon salt
¼   teaspoon coarsely ground black pepper

VEGETABLES

3   large all-purpose potatoes (about 1½ pounds total), unpeeled, cut lengthwise into ½-inch-thick slices
2   tablespoons fresh lemon juice
1   tablespoon olive oil
4   small zucchini (about 6 ounces each), each cut lengthwise into 3 pieces
3   medium heads Belgian endive, each cut lengthwise in half
2   large red peppers, each cut lengthwise in half, stems and seeds removed
1   large yellow pepper, cut lengthwise in half, stem and seeds removed
2   bunches green onions
2   tablespoons chopped fresh parsley for garnish

1. Prepare Bagna Cauda: In small bowl, with wire whisk, combine oil, anchovies, garlic, lemon peel, salt, and pepper; set aside. Makes ½ cup.

2. In deep 12-inch skillet, heat potato slices and enough water to cover to boiling. Reduce heat to low; cover and simmer until tender, 8 to 12 minutes. With slotted spoon, remove potatoes to paper towels to drain; pat dry.

3. Prepare outdoor grill for direct grilling over medium heat.

4. In small bowl, mix lemon juice and oil. Brush cooked potato slices and other vegetables with lemon-juice mixture on 1 side. Grill vegetables in batches, turning over once and brushing with remaining lemon-juice mixture, until browned and tender, 5 to 15 minutes, depending on the vegetable.

5. Transfer vegetables to large platter as they are done. Stir Bagna Cauda and pour over vegetables. Sprinkle with parsley for garnish.

EACH SERVING: About 200 calories, 4g protein, 18g carbohydrate, 7g total fat (1 saturated), 2mg cholesterol, 195mg sodium

Grilled Vegetable Stacks

These colorful vegetable "napoleons" can be served hot, warm, or at room temperature. If you like, grate Parmesan cheese over each stack before serving or set out in a bowl for self-serve.

PREP: 20 minutes   **GRILL:** 8 to 13 minutes
MAKES: 4 main-dish servings

wooden toothpicks or bamboo skewers

1   medium red onion, cut into 1/2-inch-thick slices

2   medium zucchini and/or yellow summer squashes, cut diagonally into 1/2-inch-thick slices

1   large yellow or red pepper, stems and seeds removed, cut lengthwise into quarters

1   medium eggplant (1 1/2 to 2 pounds), cut diagonally into eight 1/2-inch-thick slices

3   tablespoons olive oil

1/2   cup balsamic vinegar

1/2   teaspoon crushed red pepper

1/2   teaspoon salt

4   plum tomatoes, each cut lengthwise in half

8   large fresh basil leaves

3/4   pound fresh mozzarella cheese, thinly sliced

basil sprigs for garnish

1. Prepare outdoor grill for covered direct grilling over medium heat.

2. Soak toothpicks in water for 10 minutes. Insert two toothpicks horizontally through center of each onion slice to hold rings together.

3. In large bowl, toss onion, zucchini, yellow pepper, and eggplant with oil; set aside.

4. In microwave-safe 2-cup liquid measuring cup, combine vinegar, crushed red pepper, and salt. Heat vinegar mixture in microwave oven on High 2 to 3 minutes or until reduced to 1/4 cup.

5. Place onion, zucchini, yellow pepper, and eggplant on hot grill rack. Place tomatoes, cut sides down, on same rack. Cover grill and cook all vegetables until grill marks appear on vegetables and they begin to soften, 4 to 5 minutes. Turn over; brush with vinegar mixture. Cook, covered, until tender, 4 to 8 minutes longer, transferring vegetables to platter as they are done.

6. Assemble vegetable stacks: Remove toothpicks from onion slices. In center of each of 4 dinner plates, place 1 eggplant slice. Top each with one-fourth of onion, zucchini, yellow pepper, tomatoes, basil leaves, and mozzarella to make 4 equal stacks. Top each stack with another eggplant slice. Drizzle any juices over and around stacks. Garnish with basil sprigs.

EACH SERVING: About 445 calories, 19g protein, 29g carbohydrate, 29g total fat (13g saturated), 66mg cholesterol, 370mg sodium

Grilled Vegetarian Burritos

To make this all-in-one entrée, roll grilled onion, peppers, and zucchini in tortillas with shredded cheeses. If you prefer your burritos mild, substitute Monterey Jack without jalapeño chiles or use all Cheddar cheese. Serve with your favorite bottled salsa and a dollop of sour cream. Burritos may be cut into bite-size portions and served as appetizers.

PREP: **25 minutes**   GRILL: **16 to 21 minutes**
MAKES: **4 main-dish servings**

4	teaspoons vegetable oil
1	teaspoon chili powder
1	teaspoon ground cumin
½	teaspoon salt
¼	teaspoon coarsely ground black pepper
2	medium zucchini (about 10 ounces each), cut lengthwise into ¼-inch-thick slices
1	large onion (12 ounces), cut into ½-inch-thick slices
1	medium red pepper, stem and seeds removed, cut into quarters
1	medium green pepper, stem and seeds removed, cut into quarters
4	(10-inch) flour tortillas
2	ounces sharp Cheddar cheese, shredded (½ cup)
2	ounces Monterey Jack cheese with jalapeño chiles, shredded (½ cup)
½	cup loosely packed fresh cilantro leaves
	bottled salsa (optional)

1. Prepare outdoor grill for covered direct grilling over medium heat.

2. In small bowl, mix oil, chili powder, cumin, salt, and black pepper. Brush one side of zucchini slices, onion slices, and pepper pieces with oil mixture.

3. Place vegetables, oiled side down, on hot grill rack and grill, turning over once and transferring vegetables to plate as they are done, until tender and golden, 15 to 20 minutes.

4. Arrange one-fourth of grilled vegetables down center of each tortilla; sprinkle with Cheddar and Monterey Jack cheeses. Place open burritos on grill rack. Cover grill and cook until cheeses melt, about 1 minute.

5. Transfer burritos to plates. Sprinkle cilantro over cheese, then fold sides of tortillas over filling. Serve with salsa, if you like.

EACH SERVING: About 330 calories, 11g protein, 43g carbohydrate, 14g total fat (4g saturated), 15mg cholesterol, 655mg sodium

GUIDE TO GRILLING VEGETABLES

Preheat grill to medium-high.

VEGETABLE (4 SERVINGS)	PREPARATION	SEASONING	GRILLING TIME
8 ears corn	Soak 15 minutes, then remove silk from tops only or remove husks and silk	Brush with 1 tablespoon oil	20 to 30 minutes, with husks 12 to 15 minutes, turning occasionally, without husks
1½-pound eggplant	Cut crosswise into ½-inch-thick slices	Brush with ¼ cup oil	11–13 minutes per side
4 heads Belgian endive	Cut lengthwise in half	Brush with 1 tablespoon oil	10–12 minutes per side
2 medium fennel bulbs (1 pound each)	Cut lengthwise into ¼-inch-thick slices	Brush with 4 teaspoons oil	6–8 minutes per side
6 medium leeks	Remove dark green tops; blanch 1 minute and cut lengthwise in half	Toss with 1 tablespoon oil	11–13 minutes per side
8 ounces large white mushrooms	Trim and thread onto skewers	Brush with 2 teaspoons oil	20 minutes per side, turning several times
4 large portobello mushrooms (about 1 pound)	Remove stems	Brush with 4 teaspoons oil	15 minutes per side
4 medium red or white onions	Cut crosswise into ½-inch-thick slices; secure with toothpicks	Brush with 4 teaspoons oil	12–14 minutes per side
2 bunches small green onions	Trim root ends and tops	Toss with 4 teaspoons oil	2–4 minutes, turning several times
4 red, green, or yellow peppers	Cut lengthwise into quarters; discard stems and seeds.	No oil necessary	10–12 minutes per side
2 heads radicchio (12 ounces each)	Cut lengthwise into quarters	Brush with 2 tablespoons oil	5 minutes per side
4 medium yellow squash or zucchini (8 ounces each)	Cut lengthwise into ¼-inch-thick slices	Brush with 4 teaspoons oil	5 minutes per side
4 medium tomatoes (6 to 8 ounces each)	Cut crosswise in half	Brush cut sides with 2 tablespoons oil	14–17 minutes per side
1 pint cherry tomatoes	Thread onto skewers	Brush with 2 teaspoons oil	5–7 minutes per side

Hot Buttered
Chili-Lime Corn

Serve sweet corn hot off the grill already buttered and seasoned.

PREP: 15 minutes   GRILL: 12 minutes
MAKES: 4 side-dish servings

4   ears corn, husks and silk removed,
     and each ear cut crosswise in half
heavy-duty foil
2   tablespoons butter or margarine, softened
1   teaspoon chili powder
½   teaspoon salt
½   teaspoon freshly grated lime peel
lime wedges (optional)

1. Prepare outdoor grill for direct grilling over medium heat.

2. Layer two 20″ by 18″ sheets heavy-duty foil to make a double thickness. Place corn on center of foil. In cup, stir butter, chili powder, salt, and lime peel until blended. Dot mixture on corn and bring short ends of foil up and over ingredients; fold two times to seal well. Fold remaining sides of foil two times to seal in juices.

3. Place foil packet on hot grill rack. Cook corn, turning once halfway through, 12 minutes.

4. Before serving, with kitchen shears, cut an X in top of packet to let steam escape, then carefully pull back foil to open. Serve with lime wedges, if you like.

EACH SERVING: About 115 calories, 3g protein, 17g carbohydrate, 5g total fat (4g saturated), 31mg cholesterol, 242mg sodium

Corn on the Cob
with Molasses Butter

Cayenne pepper and coriander add kick to this molasses-sweetened butter.

PREP: 10 minutes   GRILL: 12 to 15 minutes
MAKES: 8 side-dish servings

2   tablespoons butter or margarine, softened
1   teaspoon light (mild) molasses
½   teaspoon ground coriander
½   teaspoon salt
pinch ground red pepper (cayenne)
8   ears corn, husks and silk removed

1. Prepare outdoor grill for covered direct grilling over medium-high heat.

2. In small bowl, with fork, stir butter, molasses, coriander, salt, and ground red pepper until well combined.

3. Place corn on hot grill rack. Cover grill and cook corn, turning frequently, until brown in spots, 12 to 15 minutes.

4. Transfer corn to platter; spread each ear with molasses butter.

EACH SERVING: About 105 calories, 3g protein, 18g carbohydrate, 4g total fat (2g saturated), 8mg cholesterol, 186mg sodium

Campfire Corn with Herb Butter

Roasting brings out the nutty flavor of fresh corn on the cob, and leaving the husks on prevents the delicate kernels from drying out. For an added taste treat, serve the corn with wedges of lemon or lime; the tart citrus flavor complements the sweetness of the corn.

PREP: 15 minutes plus soaking
GRILL: 20 to 30 minutes

MAKES: 6 side-dish servings

6   medium ears corn, with husks and silk
6   (8-inch) pieces kitchen twine
1   medium shallot, minced
3   tablespoons butter or margarine, softened
2   tablespoons minced fresh parsley
1   teaspoon minced fresh tarragon
1   teaspoon freshly grated lemon peel
½   teaspoon salt
1⅛   teaspoons ground black pepper

1. Prepare outdoor grill for direct grilling over medium heat.

2. Gently pull husks three-fourths of way down on each ear of corn; remove silk. In large saucepot, place corn with husks and kitchen twine. Add *water* to cover; soak for at least 15 minutes. (This helps keep husks from burning on grill.)

3. Meanwhile, in small bowl, stir shallot, butter, parsley, tarragon, lemon peel, salt, and pepper. Let stand at room temperature up to 20 minutes or refrigerate overnight, if you like.

4. Drain corn well. With pastry brush, brush each ear with butter mixture. Pull husks up and, with twine, tie at top of ears.

5. Place corn on hot grill rack. Grill, turning occasionally, until husks are brown and dry and kernels are tender, 20 to 30 minutes.

EACH SERVING: About 140 calories, 3g protein, 20g carbohydrate, 7g total fat (4g saturated), 16mg cholesterol, 252mg sodium

THE SWEETNESS OF SUMMER CORN

Fresh local corn hits its stride from July through September in most regions. But Florida ships its Supersweets nationwide all year. These have a longer shelf life than other varieties and are better able to withstand travel because their sugar takes longer to turn to starch (approximately ten days from harvest time, as long as the ears are kept well chilled). The Southern Supersweet Corn Council recommends husking and rinsing ears, then storing them in an airtight container or plastic bag in the fridge if you're not eating them right away.

No matter which variety you buy, look for tightly wrapped, bright-green husks and plentiful, golden-brown tassels at the top that are not dried out. It's not necessary to pull a husk all the way down to examine the kernels—you can feel for plumpness through the inner husk, or peek under it near the top to make sure there are full rows of kernels. They should be glossy, with no spaces in between.

Grilled Eggplant with Feta and Fresh Mint

We love the combination of smoky grilled eggplant and tangy feta cheese. Serve with grilled lamb chops for a zesty, Mediterranean-inspired meal. For photo, see page 122.

PREP: 10 minutes   GRILL: 8 to 10 minutes
MAKES: 6 side-dish servings

1   large eggplant (about 1½ pounds), cut into ½-inch-thick slices
2   tablespoons olive oil
¼   cup crumbled feta cheese
2   tablespoons chopped fresh mint
orange wedges

1. Heat a ridged grill pan over medium-high until hot. Brush each eggplant slice with oil.

2. Place eggplant slices on hot pan; cook until tender, 8 to 10 minutes, turning over once. Transfer to platter.

3. Sprinkle with feta and mint, and drizzle with juice from 1 orange wedge. Garnish with remaining orange wedges.

EACH SERVING: About 105 calories, 3g protein, 9g carbohydrate, 7g total fat (2g saturated), 8mg cholesterol, 110mg sodium

Grilled Fennel

Fennel is an interesting change from the usual grilled vegetables. Its anise flavor pairs well with steak and pork.

PREP: 5 minutes   GRILL: about 10 minutes
MAKES: 4 side-dish servings

2   large fennel bulbs (1¼ pounds each)
1   tablespoon olive oil
¼   teaspoon salt
¼   teaspoon coarsely ground black pepper

1. Prepare outdoor grill for covered, direct grilling over medium heat. Trim tops from bulbs and cut each bulb into 8 wedges. Place in microwave-safe large bowl. Cover with vented plastic wrap. Microwave on High 5 minutes. Drain liquid from bowl. (Fennel can be microwaved up to 1 day ahead and refrigerated.)

2. In same bowl, toss fennel with oil and sprinkle with salt and pepper. Place fennel on hot grill rack. Cover grill and cook fennel until lightly charred and tender, about 10 minutes, turning over once.

EACH SERVING: About 95 calories, 3g protein, 15g carbohydrate, 4g total fat (1g saturated), 0mg cholesterol, 250mg sodium

Grilled Plum Tomatoes

Be sure to use plum tomatoes. They are firm, with low moisture content, and hold up well when grilled.

PREP: 10 minutes   **GRILL:** 8 to 10 minutes
MAKES: 8 side-dish servings

8   large plum tomatoes (about 2 pounds),
     cored and each cut lengthwise in half
2   tablespoons olive oil
½   teaspoon salt
¼   teaspoon ground black pepper

1. Prepare outdoor grill for covered direct grilling over medium-high heat.

2. In large bowl, toss tomatoes with oil, salt, and pepper.

3. Place tomatoes on hot grill rack. Cover grill and cook tomatoes until they begin to char and soften, 8 to 10 minutes, turning over once.

EACH SERVING: About 50 calories, 1g protein, 5g carbohydrate, 4g total fat (1g saturated), 0mg cholesterol, 155mg sodium

Crumb-Topped Tomatoes

You can't get the bread crumbs crusty on the grill, so brown them ahead of time in a skillet. The crumbs may be prepared up to a day ahead and refrigerated. These would make the perfect accompaniment to Grilled Halibut with Fresh Dill (page 106) or Red-Wine and Rosemary Porterhouse (page 77).

PREP: 15 minutes   **GRILL:** 8 to 10 minutes
MAKES: 8 side-dish servings

2   tablespoons butter or margarine
1   cup fresh bread crumbs (about 2 slices firm
     white bread)
1   garlic clove, crushed with garlic press
2   tablespoons chopped fresh parsley
½   teaspoon salt
½   teaspoon coarsely ground black pepper
8   ripe large plum tomatoes

1. Prepare outdoor grill for direct grilling over medium heat.

2. In 10-inch skillet, melt butter over low heat. Add crumbs and cook, stirring, until lightly browned. Stir in garlic; cook 30 seconds. Remove from heat; stir in parsley, salt, and pepper.

3. Cut each tomato horizontally in half. Top each half with crumb mixture. Place tomatoes on hot grill rack and grill until hot but not mushy, 8 to 10 minutes.

EACH SERVING: About 40 calories, 1g protein, 3g carbohydrate, 3g total fat (2g saturated), 8mg cholesterol, 191mg sodium

Rubs, Sauces, and Salsas

Flame and flavor go together, and there are so many ways to add it when you're grilling. Spice rubs massaged into meat, fish, and poultry add a deep extra layer of flavor, and sauces and salsas will bring your meals to life.

Sweet Ginger Rub

Use every last bit of this on 1 1/2 to 2 pounds of steak. Serve extra soy sauce on the side.

PREP: **2 minutes**
MAKES: **about 5 tablespoons**

2   tablespoons soy sauce
1   tablespoon Chinese five-spice powder
1   tablespoon brown sugar
1   teaspoon ground ginger
1   teaspoon salt
1/2 teaspoon ground red pepper (cayenne)
1/2 teaspoon Asian sesame oil

In cup, stir all ingredients together. Rub full amount all over steak before grilling. If not using right away, store rub in tightly sealed container in a cool, dry place up to 6 months.

EACH TABLESPOON: About 25 calories, 0.5g protein, 5 carbohydrate, 1g total fat, 0mg cholesterol, 827mg sodium

Spicy Peppercorn Rub

Our simple salt-free blend works well for steak, pork, chicken, or lamb. We like to pat 2 tablespoons on a 1- to 2-pound steak—use more or less, depending on the meat's thickness.

PREP: **10 minutes**
MAKES: **about 1/2 cup**

3   tablespoons coriander seeds
3   tablespoons cumin seeds
3   tablespoons fennel seeds
1   tablespoon whole black peppercorns

Spoon coriander seeds, cumin seeds, fennel seeds, and peppercorns into zip-tight plastic bag. Place kitchen towel over bag and, with meat mallet or rolling pin, coarsely crush spices. Rub desired amount all over meat before grilling. If not using right away, store rub in tightly sealed container in cool, dry place up to 6 months.

EACH TABLESPOON: About 25 calories, 2g protein, 4g carbohydrate, 1g total fat (0g saturated), 0mg cholesterol, 7mg sodium

French Tarragon Rub

This rub has all the luscious flavor but none of the fat of a rich béarnaise sauce.

PREP: 10 minutes
MAKES: about 1/2 cup

2 medium shallots, minced (¼ cup)
2 tablespoons red wine vinegar
1 tablespoon dried tarragon
1 teaspoon salt
½ teaspoon coarsely ground black pepper

In cup, stir together shallots, vinegar, tarragon, salt, and pepper. Rub full amount all over meat or chicken before grilling. If not using right away, store rub in tightly sealed container in a cool, dry place up to 6 months.

EACH TABLESPOON: About 6 calories, 0g protein, 1g carbohydrate, 0g total fat, 0mg cholesterol, 292mg sodium

Cajun Rub

Use 1 tablespoon per pound of beef or pork, 2 teaspoons per pound of fish or chicken.

PREP: 5 minutes
MAKES: about 1/3 cup

2 tablespoons paprika
1 tablespoon coarsely ground black pepper
1 tablespoon ground cumin
1 tablespoon brown sugar
1 tablespoon salt
2 teaspoons ground coriander
1 teaspoon dried thyme
1 teaspoon ground red pepper (cayenne)

½ teaspoon garlic powder
½ teaspoon ground allspice

In small bowl, mix all ingredients. If not using right away, store rub in tightly sealed container in a cool, dry place up to 6 months.

EACH TABLESPOON: About 26 calories, 1g protein, 5g carbohydrate, 1g total fat (0g saturated), 0mg cholesterol, 1,400mg sodium

Lime-Herb Rub

Try this under the skin of a whole chicken, over a pork tenderloin, or on salmon or other oily fish.

PREP: 15 minutes
MAKES: about 3/4 cup

1 lime
1 cup loosely packed fresh cilantro leaves, chopped
1 cup loosely packed fresh mint leaves, chopped
1 tablespoon brown sugar
1 tablespoon minced, peeled fresh ginger
1 garlic clove, crushed with garlic press
1 green onion, thinly sliced
1 teaspoon salt
½ teaspoon crushed red pepper

1. From lime, grate 1 teaspoon peel and squeeze 1 tablespoon juice.

2. In medium bowl, combine lime and juice, cilantro, mint, brown sugar, ginger, garlic, green onions, salt, and crushed red pepper. Use rub right away.

EACH ¼ CUP: About 70 calories, 3g protein, 16g carbohydrate, 1g total fat (0g saturated), 0mg cholesterol, 1,195mg sodium

Chunky BBQ Sauce

Good on pork or chicken, this will keep in the refrigerator up to one week or in the freezer up to two months.

PREP: 10 minutes COOK: 17 to 18 minutes
MAKES: about 4 cups

1	tablespoon vegetable oil
1	large onion, chopped
3	garlic cloves, minced
2	tablespoons minced, peeled fresh ginger
1	teaspoon ground cumin
1	can (14 1/2 ounces) tomatoes in puree, chopped, puree reserved
1	bottle (12 ounces) chili sauce
1/3	cup cider vinegar
2	tablespoons brown sugar
2	tablespoons light (mild) molasses
2	teaspoons dry mustard
1	tablespoon cornstarch
2	tablespoons water

1. In 12-inch skillet, heat oil over medium heat. Add onion and cook, stirring occasionally, until tender, about 10 minutes. Add garlic and ginger and cook, stirring, 1 minute. Stir in cumin, tomatoes, puree, chili sauce, vinegar, sugar, molasses, and mustard; heat to boiling over high heat. Reduce heat to medium-high and cook, uncovered, 5 minutes, stirring occasionally.

2. In cup, mix cornstarch and water until blended. Stir mixture into sauce and cook until sauce boils and thickens, 1 to 2 minutes longer. Cover and refrigerate if not using right away.

EACH 1/2 CUP: About 120 calories, 2g protein, 25g carbohydrate, 2g total fat (0g saturated), 0mg cholesterol, 655mg sodium

Secret-Recipe BBQ Sauce

Pineapple adds tang to this slow-simmered sauce. Brush it over anything from chicken to hamburgers.

PREP: 15 minutes COOK: about 37 minutes
MAKES: about 5 cups

1	tablespoon olive oil
1	large onion (12 ounces), chopped
2	tablespoons chopped, peeled fresh ginger
3	tablespoons chili powder
3	garlic cloves, crushed with garlic press
1	can (8 ounces) crushed pineapple in juice
1	can (28 ounces) crushed tomatoes in puree
1/3	cup ketchup
1/4	cup cider vinegar
3	tablespoons dark brown sugar
3	tablespoons light (mild) molasses
2	teaspoons dry mustard
1	teaspoon salt

1. In 5- to 6-quart saucepot, heat oil over medium heat until hot. (Do not use a smaller pan; sauce bubbles up and splatters during cooking—the deeper the pan, the better.) Add onion and ginger; cook until onion is tender and golden, about 10 minutes, stirring occasionally. Add chili powder; cook, stirring, 1 minute. Add garlic and pineapple with its juice, and cook 1 minute longer.

2. Remove pot from heat. Stir in tomatoes with their puree, ketchup, vinegar, brown sugar, molasses, mustard, and salt. Spoon one-fourth of sauce into blender. At low speed, puree until smooth. Pour sauce into bowl; repeat with remaining sauce.

3. Return sauce to saucepot; heat to boiling over high heat. Reduce heat to medium-low and cook, partially covered, stirring occasionally, until reduced to about 5 cups, about 25 minutes.

4. Cover and refrigerate if not using right away. Sauce will keep up to 1 week in refrigerator or up to 2 months in freezer.

EACH 1 CUP: About 220 calories, 3g protein, 47g carbohydrate, 3g total fat (0g saturated), 0mg cholesterol, 960mg sodium

Horseradish Salsa

For a peppier salsa, add more horseradish.

PREP: 15 minutes

MAKES: about 2 cups

3	ripe medium tomatoes (about 1 pound) cut into 1/2-inch pieces
1	cup loosely packed fresh parsley leaves, chopped
1/2	small red onion, minced
2	tablespoons bottled white horseradish
1	tablespoon balsamic vinegar
1	tablespoon olive oil
1/2	teaspoon salt

In medium bowl, place tomatoes, parsley, red onion, horseradish, vinegar, oil, and salt; toss to combine. Cover and refrigerate up to 2 hours.

EACH 1/4 CUP: About 35 calories, 1g protein, 4g carbohydrate, 2g total fat (0g saturated), 0mg cholesterol, 180mg sodium

Orange-Chipotle Salsa

The sauce in canned chipotle chiles in adobo sauce adds a nice smoky note to salsas and grill sauces. If you don't have a can open, use chipotle hot sauce.

PREP: about 20 minutes

MAKES: about 1 1/2 cups

3	medium navel oranges
2	plum tomatoes, seeded and chopped, or 3/4 cup grape tomatoes, quartered
2	green onions, thinly sliced
1	tablespoon chopped fresh cilantro
1/2	teaspoon canned chipotle chile sauce or 1 teaspoon chipotle hot sauce
1/4	teaspoon salt

1. From 1 orange, grate 1 teaspoon peel; place in medium bowl. Cut peel and white pith from all oranges. Holding oranges, 1 at a time, over bowl, cut on either side of membranes to remove each segment, allowing fruit and juice to drop into bowl. Discard seeds, if any. With kitchen shears, coarsely cut up orange segments.

2. To bowl with fruit, add tomatoes, green onions, cilantro, chipotle puree, and salt; stir to combine. Cover and refrigerate salsa up to 6 hours if not serving right away.

EACH 1/4 CUP: About 40 calories, 1g protein, 10g carbohydrate, 0g total fat, 0mg cholesterol, 105mg sodium

Pineapple Salsa

Spiked with jalapeño and cilantro, this spicy-sweet fruit salsa turns simply grilled fish, pork, and chicken into a sensational meal.

PREP: **15 minutes**
MAKES: **about 4 cups**

1	large lime
1	ripe pineapple, rind removed, cored, and coarsely chopped
1	cup loosely packed fresh cilantro leaves, chopped
1	jalapeño chile, seeded and minced
1	green onion, thinly sliced
1	teaspoon sugar
¼	teaspoon salt
⅛	teaspoon coarsely ground black pepper

1. From lime, grate ¹/₂ teaspoon peel and squeeze 2 tablespoons juice.

2. In medium bowl, mix lime peel and juice with pineapple, cilantro, jalapeño, green onion, sugar, salt, and pepper. If not serving right away, cover and refrigerate up to 4 hours.

EACH ¼ CUP: About 20 calories, 0g protein, 5g carbohydrate, 0g total fat, 0mg cholesterol, 35mg sodium

Peach Salsa

Be patient. Wait until it is the height of peach season to make this sweet-hot salsa. Spoon over grilled chicken breasts or pork chops.

PREP: **30 minutes plus chilling**
MAKES: **about 3 cups**

1¾	pounds ripe peaches (5 medium), peeled, pitted, and chopped
2	tablespoons finely chopped red onion
1	tablespoon chopped mint
1	teaspoon seeded, minced jalapeño chile
1	tablespoon fresh lime juice
⅛	teaspoon salt

In medium bowl, gently stir peaches, onion, mint, jalapeño, lime juice, and salt until well mixed. Cover and refrigerate 1 hour to blend flavors or up to 2 days.

EACH ¼ CUP: About 23 calories, 0g protein, 6g carbohydrate, 0g total fat, 0mg cholesterol, 25mg sodium

Mango-Kiwi Salsa

The combination of mango and kiwifruit gives this salsa its sweet and tangy flavor. Try substituting chopped pitted fresh cherries and a diced yellow pepper for the mango and kiwi.

PREP: 15 minutes

MAKES: about 4 cups

2   ripe mangoes, peeled, pitted, and coarsely chopped

2   medium kiwifruit, peeled and coarsely chopped

3   tablespoons seasoned rice vinegar

1   tablespoon grated, peeled fresh ginger

1   tablespoon minced fresh cilantro

In medium bowl, combine mangoes, kiwifruit, vinegar, ginger, and cilantro. If not serving right away, cover and refrigerate up to 12 hours.

EACH ¼ CUP: About 25 calories, 0g protein, 6g carbohydrate, 0g total fat, 0mg cholesterol, 60mg sodium

Cucumber Relish

This is delicious served alongside grilled fish.

PREP: 10 minutes

MAKES: about 2 ½ cups

4   medium Kirby cucumbers (about 4 ounces each), cut into ¼-inch pieces

¼   cup seasoned rice vinegar

2   tablespoons chopped red onion

1   tablespoon vegetable oil

¼   teaspoon crushed red pepper

In medium bowl, with spoon, combine cucumbers, vinegar, onion, oil, and crushed red pepper. If not serving right away, cover and refrigerate up to 2 hours.

EACH ¼ CUP: about 25 calories, 0g protein, 3g carbohydrate, 1g total fat (0g saturated), 0mg cholesterol, 120mg sodium

Metric Equivalents

The recipes in this book use the standard United States method for measuring liquid and dry or solid ingredients (teaspoons, tablespoons, and cups). The information on this chart is provided to help cooks outside the U.S. successfully use these recipes. All equivalents are approximate.

METRIC EQUIVALENTS FOR DIFFERENT TYPES OF INGREDIENTS

A standard cup measure of a dry or solid ingredient will vary in weight depending on the type of ingredient. A standard cup of liquid is the same volume for any type of liquid. Use the following chart when converting standard cup measures to grams (weight) or milliliters (volume).

Standard Cup	Fine Powder (e.g., flour)	Grain (e.g., rice)	Granular (e.g., sugar)	Liquid Solids (e.g., butter)	Liquid (e.g., milk)
1	140 g	150 g	190 g	200 g	240 ml
3/4	105 g	113 g	143 g	150 g	180 ml
2/3	93 g	100 g	125 g	133 g	160 ml
1/2	70 g	75 g	95 g	100 g	120 ml
1/3	47 g	50 g	63 g	67 g	80 ml
1/4	35 g	38 g	48 g	50 g	60 ml
1/8	18 g	19 g	24 g	25 g	30 ml

COOKING / OVEN TEMPERATURES

	Fahrenheit	Celsius	Gas Mark
Freeze water	32° F	0° C	
Room temperature	68° F	20° C	
Boil water	212° F	100° C	
Bake	325° F	160° C	3
	350° F	180° C	4
	375° F	190° C	5
	400° F	200° C	6
	425° F	220° C	7
	450° F	230° C	8
Broil			Grill

LIQUID INGREDIENTS BY VOLUME

1/4 tsp	=					1 ml
1/2 tsp	=					2 ml
1 tsp	=					5 ml
3 tsp	=	1 tblsp	=	1/2 fl oz	=	15 ml
2 tblsp	=	1/8 cup	=	1 fl oz	=	30 ml
4 tblsp	=	1/4 cup	=	2 fl oz	=	60 ml
5 1/3 tblsp	=	1/3 cup	=	3 fl oz	=	80 ml
8 tblsp	=	1/2 cup	=	4 fl oz	=	120 ml
10 2/3 tblsp	=	2/3 cup	=	5 fl oz	=	160 ml
12 tblsp	=	3/4 cup	=	6 fl oz	=	180 ml
16 tblsp	=	1 cup	=	8 fl oz	=	240 ml
1 pt	=	2 cups	=	16 fl oz	=	480 ml
1 qt	=	4 cups	=	32 fl oz	=	960 ml
				33 fl oz	=	1000 ml

DRY INGREDIENTS BY WEIGHT

(To convert ounces to grams, multiply the number of ounces by 30.)

1 oz	=	1/16 lb	=		30 g
4 oz	=	1/4 lb	=		120 g
8 oz	=	1/2 lb	=		240 g
12 oz	=	3/4 lb	=		360 g
16 oz	=	1 lb	=		480 g

LENGTH

(To convert inches to centimeters, multiply the number of inches by 2.5.)

1 in	=					2.5 cm
6 in	=	1/2 ft	=			15 cm
12 in	=	1 ft	=			30 cm
36 in	=	3 ft	=	1 yd	=	90 cm
40 in	=					100 cm = 1 m

Photography Credits

Front Cover: Ian Garlick/Getty Images
Spine: Thomas Barwick/Getty Images
Back Cover: James Baigrie

Antonis Achilleos: 5, 46, 104

James Baigrie: 32, 51, 90, 103

Courtesy of www.barbecue-store.com: 15

Mary Ellen Bartley: 36, 38

Monica Buck: 45

Courtesy of CHEFScatalog.com: 19 bottom

Courtesy of The Coleman Company: 18

Tara Donne: 68, 97, 107, 108, 121

Miki Duisterhof: 81

Brian Hagiwara: 6, 19 top, 20, 53, 70, 79, 99, 117 (all), 122

Frances Janisch: 34, 41

Courtesy of Kitchenkaboodle.com: 12 bottom

Alan Richardson: 30, 33, 56, 86, 89, 101

Courtesy of Sears: 14

Kate Sears: 64

Courtesy of The Sharper Image: 16

Shutterstock: 27, 31, 43, 58, 73, 76, 82, 91, 93, 102, 120, 126; Teresa Azevedo: 40; Gualberto Becerra: 12 top; Jacek Chabraszewski: 63; Freddy Eliasson: 131; Eric Gevaert: 69 left; Raymond Gregory: 37; Karen Grigoryan: 75 top; Mark Herreid: 55; Dimitry Melnikov: 62; Elena Moiseeva: 116; Francesco Ridolfi: 61; Alex Staroseltsev: 69 right; Tomasz Wieja: 75 bottom; Dusan Zidar: 110

Ann Stratton: 22, 95

Mark Thomas: 2, 115

Veer: Alloy Photography: 11

Courtesy of Weber-Stephen Products Co.: 13

Index

The Good Housekeeping Triple-Test Promise

At Good Housekeeping, we want to make sure that every recipe we print works in any oven, with any brand of ingredient, no matter what. That's why, in our test kitchens at the Good Housekeeping Research Institute, we go all out: We test each recipe at least three times—and, often, several more times after that.

When a recipe is first developed, one member of our team prepares the dish and we judge it on these criteria: It must be delicious, family-friendly, healthy, and easy to make.

1. The recipe is then tested several more times to fine-tune the flavor and ease of preparation, always by the same team member, using the same equipment.

2. Next, another team member follows the recipe as written, varying the brands of ingredients and kinds of equipment. Even the types of stoves we use are changed.

3. A third team member repeats the whole process using yet another set of equipment and alternative ingredients.

By the time the recipes appear on these pages, they are guaranteed to work in any kitchen, including yours. WE PROMISE.